P9-AQB-952

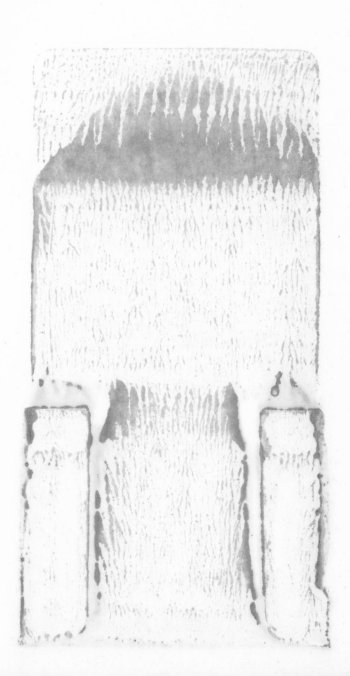

MAN IN CONFLICT

MAN IN CONFLICT

by PAUL F. BARKMAN, Ph.D.

UNITY SCHOOL LIBRARY
Unity Village
Lee's Summit, Missouri 64063
DISCARD

ZONDERVAN PUBLISHING HOUSE
1415 LAKE DRIVE, S. E., GRAND RAPIDS, MICHIGAN

MAN IN CONFLICT . . . Copyright 1965
by Zondervan Publishing House, Grand Rapids, Michigan.
No part of this book may be reproduced in any form
whatever, with the exception of brief quotations for re-
views, without the express permission of the publishers.

Library of Congress catalog card number: 65-19510

Scripture quotations marked NEB are from *The New
English Bible, New Testament,* © The Delegates of the
Oxford University Press and The Syndics of the Cam-
bridge University Press 1961. Reprinted by permission.

Scripture quotations marked RSV are from The Revised
Standard Version, copyright 1946 and 1952 by the Division of Christian Education of the National Council
of the Churches of Christ, and are used by permission.

Printed in the United States of America

TABLE OF CONTENTS

Preface

Part I
THE CONFRONTATION

1

THE RELATIONSHIP OF PSYCHOLOGY AND THEOLOGY

When I was a child, the words "confront" and "encounter" were typically used in a sentence like this: "As John walked through the woods he was suddenly confronted by a bear, and he returned home greatly shaken by the encounter." Later, when I learned more about bears, I discovered that the bear probably returned home a little shaken too.

Existentialism has put these words into the daily vocabulary of the contemporary theologian, so that on a recent visit to a theological seminary I found myself "confronted" and "encountered" at every hand. Since I legitimately lay some claim to both the theological and the psychological species, I was already aware that in such an encounter both may go home somewhat shaken, and it is sometimes hard to tell which one is most like the small boy and which one is most like the bear. Also, some on each side find me a strange and incomprehensible "half man and half beast." I trust that they will, however, find this book fit food for both species.

Rather typically, if a psychologist (of psychoanalytic orientation) were to listen to a theologian (of Calvinist orientation) discuss theology, the psychologist might be quite puzzled to find himself described as "an unregenerate soul who resists the Holy Spirit with worldly wisdom because of a depraved nature and an impenitent spirit." (Unless, of course, the psychologist were a minister's son — which many of them are.) To this he might reply that the theologian has "a paranoic personality trait disturbance with an unresolved oedipal complex, who is engaging in projection of repressed hostility toward a castrating father figure." The theologian might return home proud of his testimony, puzzled and a little shaken, and say to his wife, "Today I met a psychoanalyst!" The psychologist might well go home to his wife proud of his educative function, somewhat anxious and perplexed, and using his wife as a therapist say, "Today I met a preacher!"

The fact of the matter is that they will meet each other with increasing frequency, for psychology and theology have each had a development that makes this inevitable.

The Development of Theology

On the side of theology, the time is ripe for a consideration of the doctrine of man. The Old Testament period was devoted to the study of the doctrine of God the Father. The New Testament and Early Church period, particularly up to the Council of Nicaea, was concerned with the doctrine of God the Son. The Reformation period focused on the doctrine of salvation (soteriology) as the hot-spot of common concern. At present, the doctrine of God the Holy Spirit is at the center of common interest. In each of these ages there clustered around the central theological concern a host of related secondary issues. It is impossible to deal with the study of the Holy Spirit without also taking up, in a new way, the study of the human being upon whom He exercises His functions.

In the current phase of theology, we are in the midst of very live and lively debates about the relationship of the Holy

Spirit to the inspiration of the Bible, to salvation, and to the personality and the experience of man. Psychology, with its interest in human nature, behavior and experience, very naturally enters into these debates. In fact, it seems to have been made for the occasion.

In each phase of this theological development, the theologian has grasped upon the available tools for ascertaining and testing truth. Moses proved theology by miracles. The eighth- and seventh-century prophets added the evidence of history. The New Testament writers added the living example of Christ. From the time of the Early Church, theologians have used a great deal of philosophy and logic, which they have added in a new way to the other, previous ways of understanding God and His dealings with men. In fact logic and philosophy have become so entrenched in theology that to many people they are completely indistinguishable from theology as a separate discipline, or even indistinguishable from revelation.

To this list of tools, psychology is now offering an additional whole new armamentarium in the form of new ways of thinking, which are not illogical, yet are not logic; new classifications of personality which often ignore many of the older philosophical conceptions of man; and a new epistimology which deals with intuition in a way that is both science and art. Psychology is also suggesting that some aspects of religious behavior and experience can be objectively measured.

Psychology discriminates with surprising skill the "thoughts and intentions of the heart," so that in selected areas the astute clinical psychologist understands, predicts, and even controls what was formerly regarded as the mysterious intuitive area of the human personality. He has redefined a large part of what was formerly called "intuition" as "the unconscious," and no longer regards it as unknowable. He has some practical and usable charts of its formerly mysterious workings.

This understanding of the inner nature of the human personality is transmitted to the learner partly by rational means and partly by a clinical internship, or a personal psychotherapy or both. This gives the student a direct experience of the emotional meaning of these new terms which psychology uses. In their pastoral work, non-psychological clergymen tend to look with envy on the insight and technical sophistication which the clinical psychologist has achieved. One evidence of this is the mount of loud denial of the usefulness of psychology which is readily forthcoming from some pastors; another is the flocking to courses, graduate programs, and books in pastoral psychology. There is hardly a pastor's library in the country that does not contain one or more books on psychology; and in some libraries the books on psychology outnumber those on theology — as theology has been heretofore defined.

The Development of Psychology

Riding on the tide of rationalism and scientism, psychology during the last century impatiently shrugged off what it considered to be the shackles of philosophy, theology, and the church (which were its former home) and married itself to empirical science. There resulted an amazing and bewildering progeny of new methods, facts, systems and skills — which have already been referred to.

Shortly after the turn of the present century, psychology found itself divided into seven or more groups, called "schools," each of which battled with the rest, and each of which, like the seven men of Hindustan, had a useful understanding of some aspect of human nature and behavior which it regarded as the whole picture. None of them saw the whole man. Today, the schools are all but dead, and psychologists are more commonly clustered into interest groups which draw, in a rather eclectic manner, from whatever schools of psychology meet their needs. Thus, today we have school psychologists, industrial psychologists, learning psychologists, experimental psychologists, and a host of others. Experimental psychologists tend to draw heavily upon the behavioristic school, social psychologists tend to draw upon Gestalt, clinical psychologists are more or less psychoanalytic, and so forth.

Many of these interest groups have developed from theoretical academic backgrounds into professions, which take upon themselves responsibility for the practical day-by-day needs of living people. Each group has carved out a part of human behavior, or human relationships, as its domain. They have all applied their shiny new tools, got acceptable results, and have firmly entrenched themselves in the minds of the American population.

Elsewhere in the world their success varies from country to country. For instance, a recent report indicates that in Turkey the finest air-conditioned offices and laboratories are available to highly respected, government-paid clinical and school psychologists. In America many of the professional activities of psychologists are protected by state laws, and psychologists are deified in much the same manner as were the medieval priests, or as scientists and physicians are today. I find that when I say I am a clinical psychologist, even Christians cringe before my eyes, because they have accepted the common American image of the psychologist as omniscient.

In all this new-found skill and glory, however, there is no such thing as a single, all-inclusive, commonly acceptable psychological theory of man. It is impossible to say with authority that psychology says thus or so, for there are now not seven major schools of psychology, but there are probably as many smaller groups and theories of psychology as there are Protestant denominations.

Furthermore, it is one thing to play with theories in books and classrooms, and it is yet another thing to be as responsible for people's lives as many of these professional psychologists now have become. (Young people often discover this same relationship between theory and responsibility when their own children are born.) The time has come when a fairly large number of prominent psychologists are searching rather cautiously, and sometimes shamefacedly, in the back yards of the very philosophical and theological homes which were formerly so readily abandoned. In fairness we must point out that the abandonment occurred before the present psychologists were old enough to be a part of it.

As examples of the present trend we notice that as recently as 1963 the American Psychological Association has added, as its 24th division, a new division of Philosophical Psychology. The Society for the Scientific Study of Religion, which includes many prominent psychologists, debated for a while whether or not to apply to the American Psychological Association for admission as Division 25, but decided to join the American Association for the Advancement of Science, instead, because of the large number of members who are of social science disciplines other than psychology — and it has been accepted as an affiliate of the AAAS. There is also an Academy of Religion and Mental Health, which enrolls large numbers of psychologists.

We may take notice, furthermore, that the federal government, through its National Institute of Mental Health, is now making grants of money for the scientific study of the relationship of religion to mental health and mental illness. Also, Sigmund Koch, now in the fifth volume of his monumental A.P.A.-commissioned six-volume work *Psychology: A Study of a Science,* has returned to examine with surprising forcefulness the philosophical implications of psychology and its relationship to art and religion. Everywhere there are signs that the success of the psychologist, great as it is, has not resulted in the completely satisfying Weltanschauung — the comprehensive Gestalt — that is ultimately needed in the study of man; and many psychologists are honestly troubled by this state of affairs.

The Encounter

At this juncture we may use another analogy concerning the encounter. It is as though psychology, like a brilliant and rebellious child, had run away from home, but had now come back with a bank roll and a new pink Cadillac, and were parked somewhat hesitatingly in the alley behind father's house. Many analogous emotions might be indicated. The church, like father, sees that the boy has obviously achieved something he didn't get from home, and that is worth having. He feels guilty at having waited so long for the reconciliation, and yet he realizes that the boy is a stranger as a result of their long separation. Psychology, like the son, has everything that should indicate success, and he wants his father to see it. He loves to flaunt his independence and to be condescending; but at the same time he senses, perhaps only half consciously, that he has also lost his soul and needs father's help to find it, so he can have meaning and direction. In the analogy, as in the present relationship between the church and psychology, the father is more willing to accept the son than the son the father.

Like all analogies, the similarity to life has its limits. It may well be that the father has sought out the son, rather than the son the father.

The church's desire to use these new skills has been institutionalized in a number of organizations for the study of psychology (such as the Christian Association for Psychological Studies, and the psychology commission of the American Scientific Affiliation); in a rapidly growing number of seminary programs in pastoral psychology and pastoral counseling; in such applied expressions as the large numbers of church-sponsored pastoral counseling centers, and the new professional association for pastoral counselors which has quickly attracted a large number of members — the American Association of Pastoral Counselors. This association holds meetings, proposes to publish literature in the future, and above all, certifies its members at three levels of clinical competence.

This book is intended to bring out another analogous relationship — namely, that the family resemblance between the two and their achievements may be greater than they had suspected, and that they therefore have a very good common ground to work upon.

Some Shared Questions

As things stand at this time, it is not too hard to see from a history of human thought that out of the same spirit of our times — the same general cultural and theological development — there have grown such typical modern movements as existentialism, neo-orthodoxy, pentecostalism, sociology, anthropology, and psychology. They share, among other things, a common interest in human experience and behavior.

Nowadays, the questions which are of most vital concern to Christian laymen and theologians alike tend to be such as these: "What is man?" that is, "What am I?" "What is the nature and meaning of existence?" "What is the nature and meaning of Christian experience?" "How is God related to human experience?" "What does all this tell us about God?"

To the first of these questions psychology has a huge volume of answers. As we progress along the list, psychology becomes increasingly silent, but it has nevertheless left the theologian with materials which are relevant to the answers. I am quite sure that as a result of the present encounter between theology and psychology, the doctrine of man will never again be brushed off with the brief chapter that it has often received in earlier writings, as though it were of little importance.

1. What Is Man?

In response to the first question, psychology offers thousands of volumes, and tens of thousands of articles in learned journals. Let us take notice of several emphases that look now as though they may have a lasting impact on theology.

The first is that man is regarded by psychology as a psychosomatic organism, in which the elements of the physical and the mental are so interrelated, and so interdependent, that it is futile to try to deal with them separately. For instance, the brain is biologically inherited; it determines intelligence, which in turn determines whether a person is capable of being a theologian. It would appear that for every Christian the most spiritual of thoughts must pass through, and be mediated by this mass of fatty brain cells, and that no spiritual thoughts are possible at all when these cells and their connections are not functioning properly.

A pastor who works on a college campus and in a hospital for the mentally retarded soon finds that the nature of spiritual experience, and the type of pastoral counseling differ greatly — not because a different theology applies, but because the intellectual capacities differ.

Another example of the psychosomatic relationship lies in the finding that spiritual values and mental problems are closely interrelated with far more than half of human physical illnesses. There is a vast and growing literature about the ways in which these interrelationships operate, and the following chapters will deal partly with that literature. A recent, thought-provoking report on another kind of psychosomatic relationship indicates that in an aesthetic setting an atheistic young man was given an injection of lysurgic acid, and thereupon experienced such an overwhelming devotion that he became religious. In the light of such evidence we are likely to find that the old mind-body-spirit problem has not been at all settled, but will receive much more searching theological treatment than it has had until now.

A second important psychological answer to the question of what man is comes from the concept that man is primarily a non-rational creature; he becomes rational only with difficulty, and even then mostly at the surface. Reason may or may not be man's highest function, but at least it is far from his only normal function; and it has its own unconscious motivations deep within the personality. It is far from infallible. In fact, there are those who believe it is more often the servant of man's deeper, non-rational needs, and not nearly so often their master — even in the most disciplined of people.

This view is in some ways a direct challenge to some parts of older, logic-oriented theological concepts. The objection that this theory of the unconscious does not seem to give much help to a certain proportion of the people is no more valid than the argument that some people get nothing out of Christianity, and it overlooks the fact of the large number of people for whom this insight has been the means of mental healing which was previously not accomplished by any method. Related to this, although not a part of the theory of the unconscious, are the findings of physiological psychology with regard to the functions of the nervous system, and the place of the endocrine glands in emotion and motivation.

As this book helps to point out, there is enough recognizable parallel material in the Bible so that this matter will have to be worked through with much more thoroughness than has been done till now. Closely related to the theories of unconscious and physiological functions in motivation are problems of how the Holy Spirit communicates with and directs the activities of man. Christians have always held that such communication between man and God is largely non-rational, or extra-rational. And according to the psychologist, the non-rational characteristic of man's nature is closely related to how man finds meaning in life. The Bible seems to distinguish between man's mind and "heart," and to appeal most often to the heart. The clinical psychologist finds that a very interesting concept — the heart.

2. *What Is the Meaning of Existence?*

In response to the second question, "What is the meaning of existence?" psychology again offers its answers. For one thing, psychology uses a whole new language, which represents a detailed new way of classifying and thinking about man and his behavior. A psychologist feels quite comfortable in his evaluation of human personality, and in his descriptions of what man experiences and does. On the whole, the clergy have recognized the value of much that has been done here. Hans Hofmann says, "Psychiatry has revealed a depth of human suffering and confusion which heretofore we did not

---

[1]Hans Hofmann, ed., *Making the Ministry Relevant* (New York: Charles Scribner's Sons, 1960), p. xiii.

even think possible."[1] When this contribution is more fully explored, there may open up a new approach to the understanding of the book of Job. Psychiatrist Carl Jung's book, *Answer to Job*,[2] is at least an attempt in that direction.

The extent to which psychology has taken over the ministry of compassion may be illustrated by the words with which Dr. John Dorsey, a Detroit clinic director, is reported to have opened a staff meeting: "We must be able to identify with the maggot in the dead rat." Wayne Oates[3] says that no one has ever done so thorough a job of expounding human depravity as has Sigmund Freud. Thus there is opened up a whole new approach to the subject of sin and salvation in the Bible. It is certain that in my own life the Lord's Supper became an overwhelmingly meaningful Communion when I had spent some time in the study of personality by way of giving a number of Rorschach tests, which test is based on the concepts advanced by Freud. When I had seen at first hand what lurks in the depths of personality, and realized that my own unconscious was not essentially different from that of others, I became again what William James called "a sick soul" who is a ripe candidate for redemption, crying, "How could He love me? How great is the love that could love me!"

There are also some meaningful parallels between the biblical discussions of sin and psychoanalytic concepts of psychoneurotic illness. Dr. John Vayhinger, a clinical psychologist and an ordained minister, says:

> Both [the Bible and psychoanalysis] declare that man finds himself in inner conflict, filled with hatred, envy and mistrust. . . .
> In both man is enslaved centrally, and it is from this inner condition that particular maladjustive symptoms, or individual sinful actions,

[2]Carl Jung, *Answer to Job* (Cleveland: World Publishing Co., Meridian Books).

[3]Wayne Oates, *Religious Factors in Mental Illness* (New York: Association Press, 1955).

come. Good deeds and good intentions make little difference to this inner "root of sin" or "old man." In one, it is the effect of the original parents, Adam and Eve . . . in the other it is the effect of the natural parents . . . who set the scene for present day conflict.

In both, the injurious influences of others are so interwoven with personal reactions that they can never be differentiated. . . . In neither can the central problem be solved by "willing it so"; rather, the change must come about through radical change to the center of the personality. And in both a "helper" (or Savior) is needed, someone outside oneself but with real genuine interest, skill and hard work who can see the change brought about, and who will "accept the individual."[4]

3. The Nature and Meaning of Christian Experience.

It is evident that the answers to the previous questions have an important bearing on this question. For example, as we understand more about the involvement of both the chemical and the cognative factors in emotion, we can better discriminate between cause and effect, or between vehicle and content in certain religious experiences. This becomes rather important when we consider the Pentecostal interpretations of some parts of Scripture, and ask, "What is natural to man and what is a supernatural experience?" Right along with this, such psychological information as we have on hypnosis and psychosomatic medicine become vitally related to problems concerning speaking in tongues and faith healing. An understanding of the mechanism of conversion, as manifest in nonreligious situations, is helpful in determining the place of form and meaning in the Christian experience of this kind.

All in all, the nature of the Holy Spirit's work comes under more meaningful scrutiny as a result of certain psychological knowledge and theories. Certainly, the great amount of study in the area of mental illness must eventually be brought to-

---

[4]John Vayhinger, "Christianity and Psychotherapy," *The Taylor University Bulletin*, Vol. 54, No. 6 (February 1962), 4-7.

gether with the biblical teaching about demon possession. When it is, I anticipate benefits to both sides of the encounter. At present, psychology can at least help theology to ask more meaningful questions in these areas.

4. *How Is God Related to Human Existence and Experience?*

Although the psychologist is out of his province when we come to this question, yet he has left us with some new suggested answers, and has helped to reshape the problem for the theologian. Spirit and matter appear to be related in a new way after one has studied psychology. Even the old dichotomy of monism versus dualism seems to be an outmoded way of stating the question.

Furthermore, in its study of mental illness psychology has discovered that this mental chaos is orderly, and that falsehood has its rules as well as truth.

5. *What Does This Tell Us About God?*

The psychologist, as a psychologist, cannot and should not attempt to answer such a question. But if the theologian says that man is made in the image of God, and if God does indeed reveal Himself in His dealings with men, then the psychologist will have helped the theologian to a fuller understanding of God because he has helped to give a somewhat clearer and more detailed conception of man's nature and man's experience of God — and with God.

Benefits of the Encounter

It is not to be expected that the final outcome of the encounter of psychology and theology will result in any more of a basic change in the essential doctrines of Christianity than has resulted in the encounters of the past — nor in much less change. It is rather certain, however, that there can be a considerable change in the life and experience of the individual Christian.

The outlines which Scripture gives us may be expected to be greatly filled in with meaningful detail and supplementary material; the tested doctrines will be much expanded and clarified; and Christianity will doubtless be left with a vast, useful array of new tools with which to better conduct the godly life and the Christian warfare. I anticipate that, as a result, we will be much more able than previously to appropriate to ourselves the benefits which God intended for us to derive from our relationship to Him, to others, and to the creation around us.

At this point in our development it is important to remember that both theology and psychology are the attempts of fallible men to understand God, His creation and His methods. Evangelical Christianity does not regard either theology or psychology as divinely inspired in the same sense as the Bible, though both may be guided by the Holy Spirit if men are willing. Each has tools which are useful. Theology needs to absorb more of the methods and some of the content of psychology as it has of philosophy. Psychology needs to remember that it is a specialized and incomplete approach to the total understanding of the person, and it also needs to get back its soul and goal — a task with which theology should be asked to help.

For the present, I believe we should engage in a sort of ground work which might be called Biblical Psychology — very much like Biblical Theology — in which we attempt to ferret out the exact psychological meaning of each book of the Bible, each idea, and even each statement. If the Bible and psychology are both true, there should be important points of agreement between them, and our understanding of each should be enhanced by the contributions of the other.

Because psychology, like other science-oriented disciplines, is a growing and changing body of knowledge, we must expect that psychological insights concerning the Bible will undergo some degree of change with time. However this does not need to discourage the effort. If theologians were not permitted to develop and grow they would not publish new Bible commentaries every year. As it is, both philosophical and psychological commentaries should be written, revised, and re-written as knowledge increases.

From a variety of situations in which I have observed the encounter between psychologists on the one hand, and ministers and theologians on the other hand, it appears that one of the major sources of conflict between them is the area of method. Scientists put first confidence in the inductive method, and religionists tend largely to put their faith in deductive methods. Thus, while the psychologist wants to examine data without being prejudiced by preconceived theories, the minister wants first to know how things fit into his accepted theology.

Typically, the psychologist reads a paper on some aspect of human behavior, noting physical phenomena or observed relationships, and is satisfied to have done so. He may be quite unable to say how it fits into any larger theory. He may be quite satisfied to let the larger theory come in its own good time, or be supplied by some other scientist. He is satisfied with the feeling that, "This is what I have observed under the best methods of observation which are available to me." The minister, having usually been trained first in the systematic theology of his church, is inclined to raise the question,

"Where do you put the Holy Spirit into this?" or even, "But is this sound doctrine?" At this point there is a tendency for them to leave the room literally by opposite doors, with grave mental reservations about each other's sincerity in the quest for truth.

If one accepts the Bible as divine revelation, then there is no appeal beyond it, and therefore deductive reasoning is the only direction in which one can go from this unimpeachable source. There remain problems of interpretation, however, and the reasoning of most ministers and theologians does not proceed from the revelation itself, but from their own particular formulation of what the revelation is thought to say. The result is that practically no one studies the Bible for what it has to say. Most people study it to see how it agrees with their theology. Almost without exception, the evangelical seminaries (which may be expected to be most committed to faith in the inspiration of the Bible) and the Bible schools, begin the student's curriculum with a course in theology or doctrine. Only the rare exception has so much faith in the divine revelation's ability to communicate itself to earnest seekers as to begin with an inductive study of the Bible, leaving theology to the end of the seminary or Bible school curriculum.

Thus it is that too few religionists of the sort that profess to accept the Bible as the fully and divinely inspired Word of God ever learn to reason inductively at all. If they do not have enough faith in the inductive method to use it with respect to the Bible (where evangelical doctrine says the honest seeker would surely find truth by this method) then how could they hope to have faith in the inductive method when applied to science, where the outcomes are much less certain?

For the few who are brave enough to look a bit deductively at science and a bit inductively at the Bible, this book will be welcome, and they will not expect to find all the answers neatly packed in the summary of the last chapter.

The second part of this book, comprising the next seven chapters, takes some commonly recognized concepts of the psychoanalytic theories of neurosis and makes an attempt to try them for fit on a specific portion of the Bible — the epistle of James. It seems to me that psychoanalysis and this epistle have some very parallel concepts, and that the epistle develops them in a sequence of much the same sort that would be used by a psychoanalytic teacher of clinical psychology. To be sure there are points of disagreement and disparity. But, perhaps, by introducing Dr. Freud to Brother James (or, more correctly, to our understanding of Brother James) we may find the epistle has become more understandable and therefore more usable.

Wherever the following interpretation of either psychology or James (or the relationship between them) is not correct, I hope it will stir up enough discussion that someone will eventually come forth with a better integration.

So for the next seven chapters I will rather deliberately lose sight of the forest and start labeling trees. Wrong as some of the labels may turn out to be, at least they represent a willingness to scrutinize the specifics. Where these labels are correct, they will help the passerby to know which lumber he may usefully cut and for what purposes. I would advise the reader to proceed with the assurance that he has the author's permission to select what seems correct and usable, and to reject or ignore what does not.

Besides the sort of attempt that is made at the integration of Christianity and psychology in books like this, and the discussions of the learned societies, and even by the church clinics, I would like to propose a confrontation of another sort.

It would seem challenging and useful to set up a diagnostic and therapeutic team composed of members of the traditionally involved professions — psychiatry, social work, and psychology — and a theologian of the first rank (not a pastoral counselor, in this case). Each member of this team would examine the same mentally ill persons by the methods and tools available to his particular discipline, would bring the results back to the team for discussion, diagnosis, treatment recommendations, and would follow through with an evaluation of the treatment during and after the process was complete. It would seem that in such a crucible there would be opportunity for clarification, growth and integration which we have not often seen thus far.

I am quite aware of the practical problems involved. Each person would need to have genuine respect for the skills and personal adequacy of the others — which, in the light of present professional jealousies, is a great deal to ask. There would also need to be the kind of rapport between persons of theoretical and applied inclinations which is not often found in the relationships of theoretical and applied theologians even in the same seminary and with the same basic theological commitments. Above all, there would need to be a humility and teachableness which is rare in adults of any kind. If one may fantasy the possibility of surmounting all these obstacles, it would seem the resulting effort would be an exciting and productive travail.

There now exist several settings in which this might conceivably take place. Among them is the series of seminars now being set up for the Ph.D. program in clinical psychology at the new Fuller Theological Seminary School of Psychology. If such a team is already operating somewhere I hope the results of the encounter will be shared with the public.

Eventually, we may hope for a man of proper temperament and stature to incorporate the essence of what is sound in psychology (together with some of its specifics) into theology, in somewhat the way that Saint Augustine did with the learning of his day. That is to say, in a final analogy, that I hope for an encounter in which (to paraphrase the biblical expression) "righteousness and truth have kissed each other."

Part II
MAN IN CONFLICT

Part II
MAN IN CONFLICT

An Orientation

Luther, who was preoccupied with the theme of grace, may justifiably have regarded James as an "epistle of straw." But in our present era of concern about mass neurosis, psychology may well be the Rumplestiltskin who can be called upon to weave that straw into threads of gold.

Anxiety, personality conflict, and the resultant neuroses and psychoses are putting one out of every twenty Americans into a mental hospital some time during his lifetime, with one out of ten persons going for some kind of professional assistance from a psychologist or psychiatrist during his life.

Unfortunately, there is little discernible difference between the proportion of Christians and non-Christians who become mentally and emotionally ill. Some of the churches teach that it just can't be so, but when one counts noses, it is so. The church is generally agreed that it could be otherwise, and that it should not be so. To this I agree. But one must point out that the methods which have been used by the church thus far have not really diminished the magnitude of the stream that flows from the church into the clinics, hospitals, and professional offices. Much as one would like to say otherwise, it would be dishonest to give church people the impression that Christianity, as it is commonly preached or

31

practiced, has any simple or effective solution to the problem of mental illness. It is more honest to point to the large number of ministers and their families who are themselves obliged to look elsewhere for help with mental and emotional problems.

Rather than deny the problem, let us seek a solution. I believe the Bible does offer solutions to this problem, and that it points toward some others. I do not believe that this essay in Biblical Psychology will suddenly redeem mankind from mental disorder, but I would be happy if it made at least a small contribution toward that end. The answers in this field are neither simple nor easy; but as a confirmed biblicist, I believe there is indeed "a balm in Gilead to heal the sin-sick soul," and "he that seeks shall find."

After reading Sigmund Freud's long paper entitled, "Taboo and the Ambivalence of Emotion,"[1] it dawned on me that the epistle of James appears to have what may be a theory of how neurosis comes about, what are its symptoms, and how it may be cured; and that it seems to develop this theory in an orderly way that parallels the psychoanalytic theory at a number of cardinal points. Much of the following material is a discussion, in non-technical terms (and therefore over-simplified to some extent) of these psychological principles, and how they help us to understand what James may have had in mind. I am quite aware that the epistle was written long before Freud, but I am also aware that it was not always well understood.

Let me take you, then, through a discussion of some of the psychology of human inner conflict as it relates to mental

[1]Sigmund Freud, "Taboo and the Ambivalence of Emotion," *The Basic Writings of Sigmund Freud*, A. A. Brill, ed. (New York: Random House Inc., 1938), pp. 821-864.

illness; and at the same time on a kind of Pilgrim's Regress. In successive chapters we will trace the psychological concepts of how inner conflict breaks down the personality (or keeps it from developing); and at the same time we will trace this same kind of discussion of personal breakdown as I think I see it portrayed in the epistle of James. When we have reached the point of severe emotional disturbance in our hypothetical pilgrim, and have taken a look at his inner dynamics through both the microscopes of psychology and Brother James, we will hopefully continue both our lines of study through this pilgrim's treatment and restoration to effective emotional and spiritual health.

In this way we may begin by raising more questions than we can immediately answer. In the end we will still have unanswered questions, but perhaps a few less, and perhaps better questions.

If any reader is surprised to find a Christian writing such a study as this from the general viewpoint of psychoanalysis, let me point out that there are other viewpoints, and most of them have something of value to contribute. However, almost all clinical psychology at this time is either entirely, or in significant part, based on principles which were pioneered by the psychoanalysts — not all of whom rejected God, by the way.

This origin of clinical theory and practice is so true that there is no honest escape from it. I have sometimes observed proponents of therapies who loudly denounce psychoanalysis, and seem to be so unaware of the origin of their own ideas and methods that their denunciation of psychoanalysis is stated in psychoanalytic terminology. If all the basic psychoanalytic terms and meanings were taken out of psychology, the textbooks would be much thinner, and most therapies would be unworkable. It is regrettable that there has grown up a fad among Christian people of borrowing from a source of which they are ignorant or which they are unwilling to recognize. For myself, I prefer to build on the shoulders of my predecessors wherever I can — rather than to clamber up over their prostrate bodies.

This book does not mean to imply that psychoanalysis is the only usable therapy, or that it is the perfect therapy, or that it is the answer to the current search for the "Christian therapy." It only says that it may have something to teach us which can be usable. For the present volume I am deliberately limiting myself to viewing human conflict from this general direction, in order that we may consider what that contribution may be.[1]

I doubt that anyone believes that the entire psychoanalytic theory of personality is compatible with all of Christian doctrine about man's nature. Certainly I do not believe that, and there are points in the following chapters where it will be necessary to point to some unresolved issues. Fortunately, a theory does not need to be foolproof in order to have some value. Both psychology and Christian theology have grown in the past generation, and we hope they will continue to grow, so that presently unanswered questions may become answerable. While they are growing, we must use them as they are, as well as they can be used. It is our faith that only in heaven will we know perfectly.

Meanwhile, where else can you get an evangelical Christian tour through human conflicts and the epistle of James on a psychoanalytic buggy? So come along for the ride, and let's see what happens.

---

[1]For definition of psychoanalysis, etc., see Glossary.

2

THE DYNAMICS OF CHOICE

Although we often wish it were not so, we can never escape the necessity of choosing because nothing ever stays the same. We know this, but often we are unable to make a choice, for a variety of reasons. Perhaps we are not sure of our direction. James has a remedy for this situation, as we shall see. Or perhaps we find ourselves drawn away from our goal, troubled with conflicting desires. James also discusses this problem. But before we look at what James has to say, let us spend a bit more time discussing why choice is necessary.

The Interaction of Personality and Environment

Personality is dynamic, and is in dynamic interrelationship with its environment. No matter where we look in human life we find activity. Nothing remains constant. Everything is in a continual process of change.

From a one-celled beginning, the human body unfolds and develops into an embryo, which becomes a fetus, which becomes a child, which becomes an adolescent, which becomes an adult, which matures into old age, which withers, as James says, *"like the flower of the field."* Today it is and tomorrow it lends its lifeless body to fuel the new processes of the ongoing world (1:10, 11, NEB).

The mind of the person develops also. What is character-istic of the infant is not characteristic of the child. The adolescent finds that whereas he once recognized boys and girls by their haircuts or by the style of their clothes, the development of his endocrine gland system now gives new and emotional meaning to certain physical characteristics which were formerly considered much more casually. The mature adult looks with concern on the emotions of youth, and with apprehension at the gray years soon ahead, when the "wheel is broken at the cistern" and "the sound of grind-ing is low" (Ecclesiastes 12:6, 4). Those two young lovers whose love for each other has cooled may say, "Let's go back to the way it was before," but they find that nothing about a human being can ever be as it was before. The person is an inexorably changing individual, and everything that changes seems to change everything else.

There is probably nothing one can do which is once-for-all. Being born, a person must be nurtured or he will die. Having made a decision, he must live by it. Having eaten, he must yet eat again. Having become well he must continue to resist disease. What was adequate to resolve yesterday's prob-lems does not answer today's problems in quite the same way, because the person has changed since yesterday, and so has the environment. As much as we would like to reduce the answers to life's difficulties to simple formulas which can be applied automatically, it cannot be done. The longer and more perceptively we live, the more suspicious we become of the person who has a quick, simple, easy answer to every-thing.

Our environment changes as well as our selves. No two days are ever just alike. No two tasks are ever just the same. We face a new world literally every moment of our lives.

It is similar to the world of a moment ago, but not the same.

Because this is true, we must constantly re-evaluate and re-adjust to situations around us and within us. The Bible guides us with some clear statements that certain things are wrong — murder, for instance. The civil law clearly states that some things must be done — like buying license plates for the car. Practical necessity demands certain measures — like stopping the bleeding of a wound. There are absolutes, and there are some things which, though relative in the long run, are absolutes for us in our present situation. However, in terms of the sheer number of problems which each person must solve hour after hour and minute after minute, the situations to which there are clear-cut answers are really very few. Most of our problems involve choices between shades of gray; and new decisions usually involve elements which are at least a little different from previous decisions.

This is especially true of our desires, or as the King James Version calls them, our "lusts." (The English word "lust" is the old form of the word for "desire" which is still used in the German without special reference to evil desire. The Greek indicates that "desire" is usually the intended meaning.) Without desires we could not remain alive, and we could not serve God. They are a part of the dynamic activity of the body and mind of man, given him to meet life's situations.

Yet, in one situation a full meal is a means of life and service; in another it is gluttonous. In one situation a better job provides necessary warmth, safety, and medical care for the children; in another it makes them soft, indolent and morally weak. In one situation sex expression ruins life; in another situation it creates life. In some situations it does both at the same time. It is not possible to say that the desires for food, money, or sexual relations are either good or bad in themselves. To make a value decision requires our best knowledge, our most careful judgment, and the constant guidance of the Holy Spirit. It should be evident that we do not get the Holy Spirit in the sense that we get a marble and put it into our pocket. Rather, we live with Him moment by moment; and the having of Him is a possession only when He is involved in every ongoing decision of our dynamic life situation.

So we see that as long as we live we have never arrived. This is a disappointment to the lazy spirit, for we would rather go to an altar and "decide for Christ" once and for all. We would like to possess God once and for all, or be possessed by Him, without continuing effort. We would like to have some way of solving the problems by a simple formula — one could just say the magic words in prayer and everything would open up like it did for Aladdin's magic lamp. We would like to be able to say, very literally, "I'm on the solid rock and nothing can move me." But in this life nothing stands still, and especially are our Christian lives not standing still. We are admonished to *grow* in grace. Our progress is envisioned as "from glory to glory." The aged Paul, who had laid his hands on many for healing and the infilling of the Holy Spirit, still said, "I press towards the goal to win the prize" (Philippians 3:14, NEB), much as he had earlier said, "I pommel my body and subdue it" (I Corinthians 9:27, RSV).

Nor does anything stand still in the New Testament. Everything works energetically toward a goal. "My father has never yet ceased his work, and I am working too," said Jesus (John 5:17, NEB). Every intellectual capacity, every energy of the will, every effort of the fellowship of New

Testament believers is turned toward a constant wrestling with the evil one, trying every spirit, and holding fast to that which is good. No wonder that the first name which was given to these believers — even before the word "Christian" was used — was "followers of the Way." This was the name the first Christians gave to their own religion. They called it the Way.

Looking at our own lives, have we not each come down a long road? Isn't the analogy of the road appropriate as we look toward the future? Have we ever arrived? or has it been a Pilgrim's Progress (with steps and stages, to be sure), which is a journey on a way?

It is to such traveling people that James writes his epistle. They are people who are planning to *"go into such a city, and continue there a year, and buy and sell, and get gain"* (4:13). They are people who are called upon to *"face trials of many kinds"* (1:2, NEB) as they proceed on the Way toward the goal that Paul called the "prize of the high calling of God in Christ Jesus" (Philippians 3:14). It will become increasingly clear that James was not writing to unbelievers, but to people who were trying to be well-integrated, complete, well-balanced, and goal-directed Christians.

Let us look at some characteristics of the kind of personality James regarded as ideal.

A Picture of the Perfect Christian

When James, in the eighth verse of the first chapter, speaks of a double-minded man, he does not mean a person with two heads, but rather, to use the picturesque and penetrating language of the Scriptures, a person with two hearts.

One of the chief concerns of this epistle is that the Christian shall not be divided within and against himself, but rather that he shall be *"perfect and complete, lacking in nothing"* —

"*a balanced character*" (1:4, RSV and NEB). To this purpose he says, "*If any of you falls short in wisdom, he should ask God for it and it will be given him, for God is a generous giver, who neither refuses, nor reproaches anyone*" (1:5, NEB).

James expresses the ideal state of the Christian personality by a number of words which have a similar meaning, such as "perfect," "whole," "complete," "lacking in nothing," or other expressions which we find throughout the epistle. The psychologist has words which mean rather similar things. He speaks of "integration," "coordination," "mental health," or perhaps "goal oriented." Confronted with these words and phrases we immediately ask, "Around what is such a personality integrated? Toward what kind of goal is he oriented? Wherein does this perfection lie? What does it mean to be complete or lacking in nothing?"

The answers of the epistle are quickly forthcoming and numerous, for James might be called the apostle of personality integration. One of his statements which sums it up about as well as any is, "*. . . the man who looks closely into the perfect law, the law that makes us free, and who lives in its company, does not forget what he hears, but acts upon it; . . . that is the man who by acting will find happiness*" (1:25, NEB). He also points out abundantly how and why the actions of others do not bring them happiness. But let us be more specific about the kind of personality integration which James considers ideal.

In the opening words of his epistle, James recognizes Jesus as his Lord. Like James, Christians have accepted the personality of Jesus, as portrayed in the Bible, as the example of a perfect personality. Psychologists are generally willing to agree that there has never been a more completely integrated personality than His. We do well to remember that, according to tradition, the writer of this epistle was the physical brother of Jesus in that he was born of the same mother, and lived with Jesus for the better part of those first thirty years while Jesus was still in His childhood home. He also, according to the gospel record, had occasion to observe Jesus during at least a part of His active ministry of about three and a half years (see John 2:12; 7:3, 5, 10; Matthew 12:46). It is easy to see that James had Him in mind when he spoke of integration, and it is also easy to see the thought and speech patterns of Jesus throughout the epistle. Enough has been written about this that it needs only a mention here.

Looking then to Jesus, who looms large in the background of James's writing, we see a person who was completely focused upon God and upon the mission that God had given Him. (I believe in the deity of Christ, but in this book the focus is upon His human personality.) He says, "I can of mine own self do nothing: . . . I seek not mine own will, but the will of the Father which hath sent me" (John 5:30). Or again, "I speak not of myself: but the Father that dwelleth in me, he doeth the works" (John 14:10). Concerning those whom He came to save, He says, "For their sakes I sanctify myself . . ." (John 17:19). His whole inner being joined with His intellectual dedication, so that He could say, "My food is to do the will of him who sent me, and to accomplish his work" (John 4:34, RSV).

Later, when we have dealt with some of the obstacles to personality integration, we shall discuss good integration more fully. For the present let us quickly summarize the ideal Christian as he seems to be envisioned by James.

He is a person for whom all of life focuses upon his central object of affection, which is God Himself. Everything he does is aimed at accomplishing God's will. There is no need to drive himself to what he should do. He rather hungers and thirsts after righteousness (Matthew 5:6). His very food is to do God's will, and therein he finds satisfaction. God, God's will, God's ways, and God's work are his goal, his need, his interest, his passion, and his overriding desire. He is indeed the fulfillment of the first and great commandment; for to the thundering of Sinai which says, "Thou shalt love the Lord thy God . . . and him only shalt thou serve" (Deuteronomy 6:5 and Matthew 4:10), such a person replies, "As the hart panteth after the water brooks, so panteth my soul after thee, O God" (Psalm 42:1). He also says with complete honesty, "I do nothing of myself, but the Father who dwells in me does the works."

Such a person, as James says, finds happiness in his work (1:25). He is not torn by conflicting inner desires. He is not deflected from the happy pursuit of his worthwhile goal, for nothing attracts him very greatly except the goal which he pursues. He is not separated from God by wrong acts, nor by guilt. He is a person who walks wholeheartedly on a firm path toward a known and anticipated goal. Jesus expresses it succinctly and beautifully when he says, "If therefore thine eye be single, thy whole body shall be full of light" (Matthew 6:22).

What a wonderful condition in which to be! But is it an honest description of you or of me? Are all Christians this way? If they were thus integrated, the epistle of James would not have been written. James addresses the believers of his day (the supposedly ideal apostolic church), and accuses them of speaking out of both sides of their mouths, and pouring forth at the same place sweet water and bitter (3:11). *"Brethren,"* he says, *"this ought not to be so"* (3:10, RSV).

But it is evident from this very statement that it was so. Shall we say that it is not so today?

The epistle of James was written for those who find themselves torn within, confused by conflict and pulled about by temptations. It is intended to give such persons a deeper, more honest, and more effective look at themselves. Then, by the grace of God, who gives to all men liberally and does not scold (1:5), there are signposts to the way which leads out of this distress. Scolding personalities — including some writers of commentaries — have used the book of James as a club over the head of the sin-sick soul. But James himself in the fourth chapter points out that this may well be the way of a neurotic who seeks someone else to punish for his own inner hurt. The way of God is different.

It is important for the purpose of this study to notice the concept of God which is presented to the readers of James's letter. He is a God *"with whom is no variableness"* (1:17). Being unswervable in constancy, *"God cannot be tempted with evil"* (1:13), and it would be inconsistent of Him to tempt others away from Himself. Rather, He with whom there is *"no play of passing shadows . . . of his set purpose, by declaring the truth, . . . gave us birth to be a kind of first-fruits of his creatures"* (1:17, 18, NEB) — to be integrated like He is.

In spite of this complete, calm and effortless discipline, God is not a rigid crank, nor the sort of compulsive perfectionist whom we shall meet later in this book. But God gives generously to all who ask; He recognizes deficiency without scolding. There is a paradox in this which we will find again as the study proceeds. Like other paradoxes it has a way of taking on meaning by developing in a sort of intertwining relationship rather than by a clean logical route. Perhaps the best example of such a development is found in the writings of John. Nowhere else in Scripture is the non-logical sensibleness of the love relationship so confusing and so clear as in his writings. But we see something of this paradoxical relationship in James's epistle.

Having seen the ideally integrated Christian personality as portrayed by James, and having seen that this personality must be created and maintained in a constantly changing environment, let us see something of the process by which personality disturbance comes about.

The Lured Personality

In the article by Freud, which has already been referred to, he says that personality conflict arises when desires are at variance with an accepted standard of value. He speaks of "the inner condemnation of such acts which realized some of our definite wish impulses."[1] O. Hobart Mowrer, a currently very active and strongly anti-Freudian psychologist, agrees with Freud in this respect, but says that mental disorder is the result of trying to *live secretly* at variance with the accepted standards.[2]

Notice that neither Freud nor Mowrer have stated what these accepted standards should be. Freud has only said that, whatever a person's standards are, the conflicted personality is one that does not want to accept them. Mowrer says such a person is secretly living in disobedience to whatever his standards may be. James, however, goes farther than these men and states definitely what he regards as the correct standards.

In his opening chapter James presents us with a concept

---

[1] *Ibid.*, p. 860.

[2] See, O. Hobart Mowrer, *The Crisis in Psychiatry and Religion* (Princeton: D. Van Nostrand Company, Inc., 1961), paperbound.

similar to Freud's. He says, *"Temptation arises when a man is enticed and lured away by his own lust"* (1:14, NEB). James does not say here from what position the tempted person is lured away. He only states that this deflection from the original direction takes place. But we have already seen the original direction of the Christian which James had in mind. James envisioned a person who was walking in the Way; then came his active desires — his God-given desires, without which he could not even remain alive — and lured him aside. He does not call the luring or the being lured a sin, but he warns that under these conditions the desire *"gives birth to sin,"* which can lead to ultimate death (1:14, NEB).

Let us look at some examples of how such a luring can easily take place by virtue of the fact that each situation requires a new application of judgment and choice, a new measure of grace, and a renewed direction of the basic animal nature which does not and cannot leave us alone as long as we live.

There is nothing wrong with the desire for knowledge. If there were, then to read this book would be sin (and some people do consider it to be sin). In fact, to hear a sermon or even to read the Bible would be a sin. But it is doubtful that even the most anti-intellectual Christian would carry the argument that far. On the contrary, Hosea says of Israel, "My people are destroyed for lack of knowledge . . ." (Hosea 4:6), and the Proverbs give repeated praise to both wisdom and knowledge, which they liken to precious stones. Yet the serpent appealed to the desire for knowledge when it spoke to Eve; and there are those today who are condemned for "ever learning" and never being "able to come to the knowledge of the truth" (II Timothy 3:7).

The Scripture frequently appeals to the desire for security

— promising it as a blessing of God that every man shall sit under his own fig tree and eat unmolested of his own vine, or prophesying a millennial reign of peace. Those who work for their own security and the security of others are engaged in a blessed work. Yet Abraham was led to falsehood concerning Sarah because he wanted to be secure.

It is commendable to want the favor of those in high places. "Seest thou a man diligent in his business?" says the Bible, "he shall stand before kings; he shall not stand before obscure men" (Proverbs 22:29, margin). Yet Balaam is not the only man for whom the desire for honor has been a snare.

Almost anything that God has created within us as a necessary and wholesome desire can lure us to evil. In one situation it is good; in another it is bad. Whatever one may mean by the eradication of the old nature, it cannot possibly mean that potentially evil desires are no longer present; and it cannot mean that it is always easy to make good judgments. Every action still requires a dynamic reckoning with ourselves and the world. Each situation presents a new problem, and because it is new, the solution is not automatic.

Gold is good and gold is bad. To Achan it was the same temptation that it is to many modern Christians. Yet the church could not continue without it.

The Scripture says, "Fathers, provoke not your children to anger, lest they be discouraged" (Colossians 3:21). But of Eli and of Samuel — both wise and kind men — it says that God was against them because they did not restrain their children. Even mildness can be evil.

David's fall did not occur because sex is evil, for the Scripture abundantly testifies that sex and sexual pleasure are the creations of God, and He calls them both good. The same desire that made David the physical ancestor of Jesus also made him an adulterer.

Solomon, who asked not for knowledge but for wisdom and who received it abundantly from God, later worshiped at shrines of his own making, like any humanist of today.

All these people who started on the right way and toward the right goals found that it is not so simple as it is made to seem. They found that the very things they needed in order to do God's will could also turn them aside. They found, as we do, that much as we would like to have some kind of formalistic "eternal security" which would make it unnecessary ever to have to worry about sinning again, unnecessary to be careful, unnecessary to engage in constant decision-making, unnecessary to bear constant responsibility — much as we would like to find a formula that would give us this kind of a rocking-chair ride to heaven, there isn't any.

"My soul be on thy guard, ten thousand foes await," remains true for us. Saint Paul says he is careful, "lest . . . when I have preached to others, I myself should be a castaway" (I Corinthians 9:27). Regardless of whether we think of the seventh chapter of Romans as referring to the Christian or to the non-Christian, the fact remains that the Christian who is described in the eighth chapter is still admonished to be careful and to set his mind firmly. Evidently he still needs to. The eighth chapter still has its warnings and precautions to the Christian about what he must consciously do or avoid.

The same endocrine gland system that makes one safe in danger also makes it possible for him to be angry. If it ever becomes impossible for one to be angry, he will no longer be safe from bodily harm. The same physiological processes that function when a man is interested in the physique of one woman are ready to function with regard to any beautiful

woman. If it ever becomes impossible for him to react to
women at the physiological level, then woe to his own marriage bed as well. The same intelligence that makes a person
quick to understand truth also makes him quick to understand error.

Thus it is that a man is tempted. He is turned aside from
his purpose. He leaves the path, for the moment incautious
about where his desires lead him. He finds himself still desir-
ing to pursue his highest objective, but also drawn in another
direction. If we may assume that he comes quickly to his
senses and as quickly regains his direction, then we may
assume that all is well. But James points out that this is not
always the case, even among Christians; and our experience
tells us that he is quite right.

Thus conflicts develop. In fact, sometimes they seem always to have been present. They seem to be built into the
very way we are made. To pretend that they do not exist is
pure hypocrisy of the sort that we too often find in the
person who tells us very hotly that he no longer gets angry —
or very excitedly that she is not the least bit interested in men
as men, just as people. If we remember that James is speaking
to Christians, we do not have recourse to such a deflecting
argument as, "But this refers to people who have not been
converted."

Such a lured and hence soon-divided self, James says, is the
hotbed of death. Gardner Murphy, research director for the
Menninger Clinic, says, "The ego needs [that is, the needs of
the self — the psychologist calls the self the ego] are always
tripping one another up . . . In all serious cases conflict involves more than a practical balance of impulses; it has become a question of weighing the value of two possible selves,

one self following one course and the other self following another course."[3]

It is fascinating to watch a person in a clinical setting struggle with such a basic conflict. I remember, for instance, a long series of conversations in which I used the Rogerian method of trying to repeat to the client the emotional meaning of what he had said. The conversations ran somewhat like this:

"That cop makes me so . . . mad! I could just sock him in the jaw." At which point he made appropriate gestures.

"You feel like hitting him."

"No! No! No! I wouldn't say that. That's going too far. It's just that . . . Well, really, I guess as a Christian I shouldn't feel this way, and I really don't. We talk together a lot, and I like to draw him out."

"You feel he is really not a bad guy, and you sort of like him."

"I wouldn't say that. I think he's a stinker, but I'm a Christian and I don't think I should let myself go."

"You feel you would like to be angry with him, but it is not in accordance with what you feel a Christian should be."

". . . no! I don't see why a Christian shouldn't get mad! After all! Look at Jesus in the Temple! When a guy is as crooked and downright vicious as that guy, it's just being honest to get mad at him. He ought to be jailed himself!"

Well, enough of that. After a few hours of this, the therapist may feel a bit frustrated in his efforts to get the client to see himself, but I assure you he is much less frustrated than the person who is caught in this impossible position of being un-

---

[3]Gardner Murphy, *Personality, A Biosocial Approach to Origins and Structure* (New York: Harper & Row, 1947), pp. 301, 302.

able to accept either side of himself as correct, adequate or satisfying.

James uses the term "double-minded" to describe the soul in this kind of a conflict with itself. Psychologists speak of it as "ambivalence." Ambivalence is a double polarity, or a pull in two directions at the same time. It is often unconscious, says the psychologist, but it is none the less real. The terms "double-minded" and "ambivalent" are roughly the same, and both the Bible and the psychologist are agreed that "double-mindedness" or "ambivalence" lead to the same thing — an inner breakdown which can culminate in death.

Summary

Psychoanalytic theory points out that when an individual's desires are at variance with accepted standards of values, personality conflict arises. James points to the biblical standards, and says that when the Christian's desires lead him aside from these, there is a chain of consequences which can end in death. We have noted that these desires are in themselves quite natural, but that man is in a dynamic relationship with his inner and outer environment. This makes it necessary to face constant choices, with the continuous danger of being deflected from his originally intended course. James calls the divided self that results from deflection "double-minded." Psychologists have a similar concept of "ambivalence."

> "*Let no man say when he is tempted, I am tempted of God: for God cannot be tempted with evil, neither tempteth he any man: But every man is tempted, when he is drawn away of his own lust, and enticed. Then when lust hath conceived, it bringeth forth sin; and sin, when it is finished, bringeth forth death.*"
> — James 1:13-15

3

OUR CONSISTENT INCONSISTENCIES

The person who seeks to follow a consistent way of life finds himself constantly lured in other directions, as we have seen. It is important to realize that both the desire to go in the Christian way, and the luring to another way, take place in a single person. In all of recorded medical and psychological history there are perhaps less than two hundred cases of "multiple personality" such as described in *Three Faces of Eve.* For millions of other people the conflict takes place in such a way that the personality remains largely unified, though confused.

The Unity of Personality

There is a surprising degree of orderliness in the universe, whether one is dealing with pie, mathematical probability, or personality. This orderliness is as gratifying to most lay Christians, as it is to the scientist.

If someone is eating dessert at your home, and looks up after a mouthful of pie to say to the hostess, "This is very good pie," the hostess is not likely to say, "How do you know? You have eaten only a very small part of it." Besides being more courteous than to say such a thing, she knows that from one mouthful a discriminating eater can usually tell all about the whole pie. He has tasted the pieces of apple, the crust, and the flavor of the syrup. He is likely to find very few surprises if he eats the rest of the pie.

Indeed, if one has learned the rules which govern any area of our existence, he can analyze and make predictions concerning that area with an accuracy that is limited primarily by the completeness of his knowledge of the rules. It is the assumption of science that such rules underlie all matter and behavior. Even when we deal with what one might call "pure chance," we find that randomness follows rules. The professor who constructs a multiple-choice test, each question of which has four choices for the correct answer, finds that it is impossible to vary the position of the correct answer in such a way that the student can never guess the answers. The student always has at least one chance in four of getting the right answer even if he knows nothing about the matter covered by the test. This is true if the professor uses a coin, or some similar device to decide the position of the answers. If he tries to determine their position by himself without any such randomizing device, he will produce a pattern that is not at all random, but typical of his way of thinking. The really discriminating student can soon learn the professor's pattern and correctly guess a good deal better than one chance out of four.

This is because people are a great deal more predictable than chance. There is a unity of personality which one observes whenever one deals discriminatingly with people, and which has been noted by James when he says, *"A double minded man is unstable in all his ways"* (1:8). The New English Bible translates it, he *"never can keep a steady course."* Although, as we shall see, the psychologist has much to fill in between the lines at this point, it is important to notice that James is not only pointing to a confusion of personality which results from double-mindedness, but also to the fact that this confusion has a certain orderliness or predictability about it.

James says that when such instability exists, it does not affect a part of the personality, but *all* of it. And this is a very important observation. From it we could predict that a person who is consciously aimed in one direction (performing the will of God), but is lured in another direction (a normal desire which in this case would not fulfil a righteous purpose), will likely find his action the result of the pull of these two vector forces — he will finish somewhere between the two. James also points out that on the way toward this compromise outcome (unsatisfactory to both of his motives) he is likely to travel, not on a straight course, but on a meandering route that responds first to one pull and then to the other. If this may seem to be a kind of common-sense observation, it is nevertheless a good one. This man's course, though typical of him, is neither straight nor steady.

In psychology we speak of the unity of personality. We are accustomed to evaluate personality from very small samples. For instance, there are intelligence tests. These take no more than an hour or two to administer, but from them we make predictions with a certain degree of confidence about a person's behavior, and even about some aspects of the rest of his life.

A young couple with an adopted son came recently to discover if their fond estimate of his capacity had foundation in reality. After two sessions with a little restless three-year-old bundle of charming activity, I was able to tell them with the confidence that comes from research and experience that they had better plan for a long and expensive education, because this boy is intellectually capable of earning a doctor's degree in any field that will interest him, or of being a person of responsibility in most of the fields of modern endeavor. Whether or not he will achieve to the extent of his intellectual capacity may well depend on the attitudes his parents take, but statistics gathered over generations of subjects, totaling hundreds of thousands of cases make it a fairly safe prediction. In some ways, then, we can predict what a three-year-old will be like forty or sixty years hence simply by spending an hour and a half with him, using the correct tools.

We also give personality tests. Although these are generally not as valid as the tests of capacity and of ability, yet it is possible to make important correct decisions about people. Once again, the past success of these bits of sampling of people have indicated that they are useful. (The loud cries against personality testing which one hears in some quarters are directed against the people who try to make them say more than they are designed to say or who use them unwisely for their own selfish purposes.) The very fact that we can do behavior sampling at all is based on the validated theory that personality, a little like pie, can be sampled with reasonable accuracy from no more than a mouthful.

The most surprising of these personality assessment techniques for laymen is one in which the subject is asked to look at some ink blots and report what he sees — what they look like. Since they are not representations of anything that one has ever seen or that exists, the only way a person can respond is to interpret these blots according to the way he customarily approaches things. That is to say, he must respond in a manner typical of his own inner nature, rather than in a manner which is prescribed by the visual object before him. The results are, of course, very complex, and require much training and skill to interpret, but the following joke, which is passed around among psychologists has a great deal of understandable truth about it.

The story is told of a person who went through the procedure of looking at these ink blots and reporting to the examiner what he saw — and what he saw tended to be rather racy. A few days later he is said to have approached the psychologist with the request, "Say, doc, could you lend me those sexy pictures for a few days? I'd like to show them to a buddy of mine."

Any layman can begin to interpret some things about this man's personality from even this small amount of information. He is preoccupied with sex, and he tends to see things in his environment which are really inside himself. Thus any layman could predict some very important things about the unrealistic attitudes this man would have in some situations, and he can also be sure that if this man ever sees things in an unrealistic way it is going to be pretty hard to convince him that they aren't that way, etc., etc., etc.

Although you may not be a psychologist, and probably have never administered or interpreted an intelligence test or a personality evaluation procedure, I am sure that you, too, have at some time decided that one mouthful of a person was more than enough. You needed no further sampling to know that you wished to have no more to do with such a person. Or, it may have gone the other way. People do fall in love with others at first sight. In such a case a person follows up such a first reaction with as many and as extended samplings as possible. If repeated contacts cool one's ardor, he can often think back to the elements in the first encounter which might have been clues to the flaws discovered later — if one had been more perceptive.

Indeed, the very inconsistencies of people tend to be consistent. (And that is a free translation of James 1:8, by the way.) The police keep records of the details of each crime.

From these they soon determine whether certain crimes were performed by the same or different people. The more a criminal tries to "cover his tracks" by devious and ingenious maneuvers, the more recognizable his crimes become. This develops to a point where the police can sometimes predict with considerable accuracy where, when, and how the next crime will be committed by this person or gang.

To the clinical psychologist, the analysis of the ways in which people try to defend themselves from discovery by themselves and others is one of the primary skills of the profession. People hide in typical ways. The harder they try to hide, the more obvious they usually become. To the person who knows how to read these signs it is almost as transparent as the child who says, "Don't look in the third dresser drawer, because there is nothing there."

Lest someone get the mistaken notion that psychotherapists see everything and reveal nothing, one might note that in their book about training therapists,[1] Ekstein and Wallerstein show how the therapist trainee typically signals his behavior and approach in his first meeting with his supervisors. As Dr. Ekstein has sometimes pointed out in his lectures, psychologists and psychiatrists also have unconscious processes at work.

Psychologists are a long way from the omniscience or penetrating power of God. I might wish, however, that people really believed psychologists (and other people) could "see right through" them. If they really believed that, they could stop hiding. They could be their real selves — bad as that may be — and could get their friends to help them with what is really their trouble, rather than constantly decoying them off onto secondary issues.

---

[1]Rudolph Ekstein and Robert S. Wallerstein,*The Teaching and Learning of Psychotherapy* (New York: Basic Books, 1958).

If James did not think of things in precisely this way, at least he has left room for such an understanding of human nature, by a very parallel line of reasoning to that which we have seen in psychology.

The Nature of Ambivalence

To understand a little better the personality disorganization which comes with double-mindedness let us turn back to Gardner Murphy.[2] He points to four kinds of ambivalence in his thirteenth chapter.

The first has to do with the fact that most muscles of the body work in pairs which alternately pull in opposite directions. These pairs are called extensor and flexor muscles. The flexor muscles, for example, close the hand, and the extensor muscles open it. So far all is well. When, however, a person is what we commonly call "tense," an inspection of the muscles shows that they are not alternately relaxing and contracting, but are both contracting at the same time. Therefore they pull against each other. If the pull were very strong we would call it a cramp. As it is, the tense student may sit at his desk, or the tense commuter in his train depot, moving very little, yet becoming very tired. The "double-mindedness" of their muscles has caused them to work much without accomplishing anything.

"Conflict may also consist of balanced antagonistic nervous effects on the same muscle system, as in the sympathetic-parasympathetic control of heart and stomach tonus."[3] Generally, however, a dominance of one over the other soon occurs — one component soon wins out over the other — and matters go on rather normally. For instance, he says, "A strongly organ-

---

[2]*Personality. A Biosocial Approach to Origin and Structure.*
[3]*Ibid.*, p. 296.

ized affection may withstand the impact of the panic situation: 'Perfect love casteth out fear.' But, as other instances of violence show, perfect fear also casteth out love ... one autonomic component and all that it stands for achieves complete dominance over the other."[4]

The third form of ambivalence comes in response to ambiguous signals. That is, the same object says both "Do," and "Don't." For instance, the child likes candy, so the candy signals, "Do"; but his teacher has taught him that candy causes holes in the teeth which he knows will hurt him, so the candy also signals "Don't." Which choice he will take I will let you guess, for to most children this is not a serious ambivalence. But life is full of ambiguous signals which are not so easily resolved. Regardless of what people say about money, they act with respect toward those who have wealth, even though their training may tell them that wealth is evil and should not be sought after. Parents, teachers, ministers, even young men may tell girls that they should not use cosmetics; but those same men — not always young — keep noticing the girls who do wear cosmetics. Such ambiguous signals result in pulls upon the personality in opposite directions. They can sometimes be closely balanced in their apparent ethical or spiritual values, and therefore create considerable strain.

The fourth kind of ambivalent situation is one in which subjective values are in conflict. In this case it is not the outer situation that punishes or rewards; the conflict is within us. The question is not only "What is the correct response?" but "What do I really want?" As Murphy says, "In all serious cases conflict involves more than a practical balance of impulses; it has become a question of weighing the value of two possible

---

[4]*Ibid.*, p. 297.

selves, one self following one course and the other self following another course."[5]

This can take several forms. One can want two legitimate but mutually exclusive objects. "Do I want Jane or Joan?" To have one he must give up the other, though both are good. It can take the form of a choice between two unpleasant alternatives. "If I don't get up early I will arrive after the fish have stopped biting. If I do get up early — well, who wants to get up early?" Or, again, it can take the form of loving and hating the same object. People of all kinds have said about each other, "I can't get along with him and I can't get along without him." In each of these, if I have given good illustrations, the conflict is within us. Two possible courses, and therefore two possible selves, are in conflict. This is the kind of ambivalence which most concerns the clinical psychologist, and which is most pertinent to the thinking of James.

This last possibility, of loving and hating the same person, is one of the really serious conflicts in the lives of a great number of people. Taking a rather typical example, we have the case history of a little girl whose father was not really a cruel person, but who had so many burdens of his own that when he was home he was not the warm, affectionate, supporting parent that she needed. The little girl needed to be picked up and loved and hugged. She needed somebody to play tag with her, to hold her on his lap and tell her that he loved her. She wanted these things very much, but she also knew that her father did not do these things. She excused him because she loved him and because she had been told that daddy was tired, daddy had many troubles, daddy must not be bothered because he had more important things on his mind. The more she needed his love, the greater was the hurt she felt because she

---
[5]*Ibid.*, p. 301.

was not getting it. A person has only one daddy. If he doesn't love the child, there is no other daddy to do it. (Busy preachers, take note at this point.) So he has the power to take away from that child what it needs most — a father's love. It is he who is depriving the child. It is he who is creating the great void in her life. So the need and the hurt grow together. Liking and irritation toward the same person grow together. We will follow this case later in the chapter.

Repression

Such a problem may be irresolvable for the child. She loves daddy, but in the same measure that she loves she also hates him for the deprivation which he causes. But how can one hate one's own father? That would be to lose the very person one needs most. So the problem may become too great and too dangerous to be dealt with rationally, and must therefore be pushed aside. Is it any wonder that some of you are confused in your emotions about your parents?

There are other sources of this kind of ambivalent confusion, as will be pointed out later, but notice that in this case history we have a true double-mindedness. It is also a true ambivalence in the psychologist's meaning of the term, for the problem has become so irresolvable that it has been pushed out of consciousness. For such a child there may well be no conscious problem about its relationship to the father, or, if there is some sort of consciousness about it, it takes the form of confusion.

Thus, a typical case came to me with the common complaint, "I can't think. Everything seems so confused." We discovered with time that the statement should have been, "See, I can't think, so how can I be expected to think about my problem?" This was all that was apparent to her consciousness.

Later we discovered what was the true problem, and she was able, with assistance, to tackle the conflict head-on; it was no longer necessary to maintain a state of mental confusion in order to avoid thinking clearly about the troublesome part of her emotions.

Pushing material out of consciousness is not done deliberately. It is very doubtful that it can be done deliberately. Rather, it happens unconsciously by an automatic mechanism which psychology knows by the name of repression. Although everyone seems to repress a certain amount of material (fortunately we can't remember everything we have experienced), yet repression is an important factor in every functional mental illness. It is one of the most common mental mechanisms with which the psychotherapist has to deal.

There is an important difference between repression and suppression, which should be noted here. Suppression is a conscious process, dictated by the person in the interest of some goal. For instance, the door has been slammed in someone's face, and a friend watching the behavior of the insulted person says, "How is it that you don't get angry when you are treated that way?"

To this he replies, "I do get angry, I just don't let it get control of me. I have learned how to be aware of the feeling without letting it affect my behavior too much."

This is supression. It is often difficult, but it is usually a process which is regarded as an indication of healthy emotional control.

In contrast, notice the behavior of the person who has repressed his anger. Assuming the same incident, he may indeed have made a courteous response to the same door-slamming sort of incident. The friend once again says, "How amazing that you expressed no anger!"

To this he replies, "Anger? Why should I be angry? Such things never bother me."

Now it may be true that this person does not perceive the incident as an affront; but if we find him driving home from that incident, sharply criticizing a number of people, speaking in a loud, high-pitched voice, cutting in and out of traffic in an aggressive manner, we must come to the conclusion that he has anger and is expressing it, but is unaware that he has it. In that case the anger was too threatening to recognize as a part of himself; therefore it had to be pushed out of consciousness.

Our illustration makes several things clear. One is that it is more comfortable to repress than to suppress. After all, frustrated desires, wounded feelings, or unacceptable appetites cause pain. It is so much more pleasant to be unaware of them. The other is that a person who represses doesn't thereby get rid of the feeling or memory. He just loses control of it, and it expresses itself in its own ways. These ways are often not useful for the person's good, or for the good of those around him.

It takes very little extension of this knowledge about repression to realize that some people who regard themselves as sinlessly perfect can be quite honestly convinced of this, whereas others are quite honestly aware of their glaring imperfections. The suppressor says, "I would like to but I won't." The repressor says, "I have no problem in that area."

James makes a similar observation about human behavior. In contrasting the successful, integrated person with the double-minded, unsuccessful and unhappy person, James says that the latter goes to the mirror of God's Word, "*glances at himself and goes away, and at once forgets what he looked like*" (1:24, NEB). Having seen himself in the light of his standard of values, he promptly repressed what he saw. To be sure, James does not use the word "repress," but he uses the word "forget" in such a way that it fits rather easily into the psychologist's concept of brushing knowledge aside because it is unpleasant.

This raises the question of whether something that is repressed must first have been conscious. Psychoanalytic theory holds that it may have been conscious at one time, or it need never have been conscious at all. It need only threaten to come to consciousness in order to call forth the mechanism of repression. Whether this means that the Bible does or does not recognize the repression of unconscious material cannot be decided here. What James says clearly is that there exists a state of affairs in some of his readers, in which these Christian people are not seeing themselves for what they really are. Somehow, what they read and understand about themselves doesn't sink in, but is passed off without integration into the personality. Therefore they do not get the benefit of insight.

On the other hand there are people who imagine themselves guilty of everything, or who are bothered by a sense of guilt for which there seems to be no need. This kind of false guilt arises out of an "imagined" evil act or thought, one which never in fact existed except in the fantasy of the individual. The relationship between repression and false guilt is that false guilt is often repressed (as also many other things are repressed). The result is that the personality reacts toward the repressed false guilt just the way it would toward a repressed real guilt. The argument among psychologists is about whether there is such a thing as false guilt and whether or not it does indeed form a significant cause of inner personality conflict and ultimate neurosis. The psychoanalysts insist on both; Dr. O. Hobart Mowrer denies that false guilt is involved in neurosis, and has grave doubts that there is such an experience as false guilt at all.

Other passages of the Bible are more appropriately brought into a discussion of whether there is such a thing as false guilt. Among these are the passage in Romans 7, where Paul seems to be talking about inner forces of a sort which are not under conscious control; also the opening scenes of the book of Job, where Satan is presented as a false accuser of the righteous man of God.

An example of false guilt would be that of a person who in his childhood acquired a deep sense of responsibility for the death of a parent who died in an accident with which the child had no association whatever. This is a fairly common kind of false guilt encountered in clinical experience.

My colleague, Dr. Paul D. Fairweather points out that we may be confusing terms. He contends that in such a case it is not so much the problem that the child has a false sense of guilt as that the child has a false concept of the nature of God's righteousness. One might add that there is possibly also a false sense of causation — as though the child's anger at the parent could have caused the accident for which he feels guilty.

In a sense James meets his readers at the same point where the psychotherapist meets his patient — at the point of the present trouble, not in his dim, distant childhood. Both James and the psychoanalytically oriented psychologist face the sufferer with the awareness, "There are some things hidden from your consciousness which are causing you trouble at this time." Both are inclined to be more interested in how to bring them to consciousness and deal with them than to go into the problem of how they were repressed. Blaming things onto one's childhood may be historically correct, but it is not a way in which people get healed, either in psychotherapy or in

Christian experience. In the process of getting them to consciousness, we usually also bring to consciousness how the repression came about — but that need not always be regarded as the central issue. Psychology and James agree that repression can lead to personality confusion and destruction.

James, like Mowrer, is evidently more inclined to deal with real guilt and its hazards to personality integration, and to leave the question of "false guilt" out of the discussion. He is very interested in the effects of the divided personality, and deeply concerned that the Christian shall make clearcut decisions, and live by them. He has obviously found that many Christians are not able to make such decisions and live such an integrated life, and he is aware that personality integration cannot be achieved when one goes away from insight, disregarding the true facts about one's self.

If this leaves an area of silence between James and psychoanalytic psychology, it does not need to leave an area of disagreement. The question of false guilt and of childhood sources of guilt and anxiety are not here denied. They are left open, and will appear again later in the book.

In order to take our attention for a moment off the morbid process of self-destruction which has been our topic, notice the contrasting path of happy integration which results from living by what one discovers about himself. *"But the man who looks closely into the perfect law, the law that makes us free, and who lives in its company, does not forget what he hears, but acts upon it; and that is the man who by acting will find happiness"* (1:25, NEB). Notice that the law is revealing about the one who looks into it. Notice also that the person who lives in the company of the law does not forget.

Since James talks about purposeful forgetting, rather than fading out of memory because of disuse, it may be correct to think of this as repression. Repression is purposeful forgetting, though not consciously controlled.

The way of happiness sounds simple — just face the truth about yourself and live by the biblical standards. But the fact that James needed to write this epistle is proof enough that his hearers were not finding it simple at all, but needed help.

There are some real problems with the theory of the unconscious which we cannot tackle at this time. We should notice that repression may not always be complete. Some little traces of awareness may lurk with the person, but they are so small that he says, "Surely, this little matter could not be the cause of so great a trouble as mine," and he goes on without giving it his proper attention. In a recent talk, Mowrer compared it to an iceberg which presents above the surface of the water far too little substance to seem an adequate cause of so great a shipwreck, but which when one begins to chop away at the surface, brings more and more up from underneath that surface.

Whatever the case may be, we have now built a basis for a little better understanding of James's statement that a double-minded man is unstable in all his ways.

Ambivalent Behavior

As Gardner Murphy has said, the choice which was impossible to make was not only between two alternatives, but between two possible selves. By remaining hung between them, the conflict of the inner self continues, and the whole personality (not only a part of it) is involved, even though the person may be largely unconscious of what is causing his difficulty.

Speaking of children who have been caught between irresolvable choices, Murphy says, the ". . . child may break down under the strain, losing many other well-established habit systems and showing disorganized emotional upheavals."[6] Or, again, he says concerning all ambivalent situations, "After a pattern of conflicting attitudes has been somehow woven, the unconscious, unreflecting attitude may itself be full of ambivalence."[7] So Murphy is also saying that a double-minded person is unstable in all his ways.

How far-reaching such a disorganization of the personality can be is demonstrated by several studies which have concluded that eight-tenths or more of women who have children born out of wedlock also have serious ambivalence of emotion toward their fathers. The problem, you see, has never become conscious. It is too terrible to face. Therefore the little girl of our earlier case history grows up behaving both ways at once. She finds someone who doesn't really love her — just like father. She seeks this person's love just like she pursued her father's love. The attachment is no more permanent nor satisfying than with her father. And with respect to that father she has accomplished the expression of both of her emotions at the same time: for what could she give her father of more value than a grandchild, and how could she hurt him more than to have it outside of marriage? All this is done without really knowing why. The problem has remained unconscious, but it has involved the behavior of the total personality, which has steadily followed its crooked, self-defeating course.

This is only one example of the way that the ambivalent person always defeats himself. He always loses when he wins, because a part of him is on each side of the struggle. Look at the case of the person whose emotions toward God have become ambivalent. (We shall not trace the history of such an ambivalence.) Can he love both God and Mammon without being miserable with both? (If he makes the clear-cut choice against God, then he is no longer ambivalent — and James is

---

[6]*Ibid.*, p. 299. [7]*Ibid.*, p. 302.

not speaking of such people. His fate is dealt with elsewhere in the Bible.) The clergy have been quite correct in saying that there is no one so miserable as the "worldly Christian." Even if there were no important truth in Christianity at all, the conflict between the two possible selves which Christianity forces upon us must be resolved for the professing Christian, or it will disintegrate one's personality. It is not only a question of whether our concepts of God and of God's will are correct. It is also a matter of making our choices and not trying to ride with one foot on two horses.

Students at a certain Christian college were surprised and puzzled by the behavior of a missionary's son. This school has rather conservative and somewhat demanding rules of Christian conduct. Before a student can be admitted he must read the statement of rules and sign the agreement to abide by them as long as he is in school. This young man did so, and then proceeded to flaunt the rules all over the place. This may not be too puzzling, since some young people go to a college under pressure from their parents and then express their displeasure by treating the school like they wish they dared treat their parents.

This young man was brought before the student court, which in that college deals with the enforcement of many of the rules. The court recommended to the dean of students that the offender be dismissed from school for the remainder of the year, and the dean followed the recommendation.

So far, we have little more than the usual complexity of behavior. The point at which his colleagues expressed their bewilderment to me was when the student applied to be admitted to the same school the following year, but, as far as they could tell, with no basic change in attitudes.

In light of what we have already said about the conflict

between two selves, we can see how much this fellow needed to stay in a situation where he could continue the conflict — where he could be two things at the same time. He needed to identify with the Christian way of life. He also needed to rebel against it, and he needed a setting in which he could continue to be both unhappy selves at the same time without making a permanent decision.

Consider how unhappy is the person who says both, "Well, shouldn't one be a good neighbor and self-respecting?" and, "But if I took seriously what the Bible says, I would have to go against this thing which my neighbors expect of me." How unhappy is the person who tries not to take religion too seriously, but not to leave it entirely! How confused is the person who tries to put off his decisions until later! Even going to church is a strain, because it keeps the conflict before him. Contrary to the currently popular beautiful billboards that say, "Go to church and leave your troubles there," going to church makes the troubles worse for such a person. The very God to whom he should be able to turn for help has become a source of conflict.

Gardner Murphy says, "A basic quality of human conflict is to make contact with something without touching it, to move toward it and keep away from it at the same time."[8]

He reminds us of the cat in Guthrie's experiment which had learned that by backing against a certain pole it could get free from the cage, but it would also be punished for touching it. The cat backed at the pole thirty-nine times without actually touching it. How much this is like the human being who cannot make up his mind. Wanting and not wanting. Lured and conscience-stricken. Lusting and repenting. Never quite enjoying, yet never quite leaving it alone. In the resulting confusion

---

[8]*Ibid.*, p. 302.

his whole personality becomes involved. Well may such a person cry out with the Apostle Paul, "Wretched man that I am! who shall deliver me . . .?" (Romans 7:24).

James has some answers to that question as well as does Paul, but first we must see more of the problem, and understand it even more clearly.

Before leaving this chapter it becomes necessary to mention what may be a distinction between the psychoanalytic theory of neurosis and the treatment of double-mindedness by James. Although James does talk about forgetting, and may or may not have had some concept of the so-called "unconscious" operation of forces within the personality, he seems not to deal specifically with several elements which are included in the psychoanalytic theory.

One of these with which he seems not to deal, so far as I can judge, is the matter of repression of early childhood materials that occurred before the infant could really be aware of them in such a way as to deal with them consciously. Psychoanalysis makes a great deal of these early childhood experiences, and feels that much neurosis begins there. It leaves room for later childhood and adolescent sources of neurosis, however, and does not completely rule out some slight possibility of a neurosis resulting from adult experiences — although this adult source is regarded as very doubtful. There is plenty of room for adult experiences which precipitate earlier tendencies, however. That is, the emotional weakness already built into the personality during childhood may not result in an actual neurotic manifestation until some adult experience becomes so difficult that the normal defenses of the personality break down.

These early established tendencies of the personality and early conflicts can later find expression in some religious experience or problem in such a way that the adult religious problem acts as a camouflage. The young man who has just been described might well think that his real problem was how to get along in a Christian school whose rules he regarded as being too strict, when actually this was only the most recent expression of a problem which went much farther back in his life. Christians are too frequently satisfied with looking only at the current expression of the problem, and believing that to settle this present problem settles the basic issues.

Thus I can think of several cases that have come to me where the therapy began with a discussion of a religious problem — for instance, "I can't believe in God any more" — but soon moved on to discover that behind this was a family problem of much older standing. In one instance it was the delicate task of the client and the therapist to untangle what at first looked like a wholesome conversion experience. It appeared, however, that this person had discovered a God who could let her continue to feel the same kind of conflict and anger which had earlier been repressed about her family.

At this point someone may get concerned and wonder if the therapy merely "explained away" her religious experience. Far from doing that, it left her a real love for God, a genuine commitment to His Way, the ability to use the resources she had in Christ — but left them uncluttered by those earlier per-plexing conflicts which had become tangled up with her faith at the unconscious level.

Unfortunately, not all cases arrive at the golden end of the rainbow. If I have dealt with a minister's wife who could once again go to church without vague and distressing un-easiness, I have also seen another who ended therapy at a point where the insight into her distress was merely a threatening possibility rather than a relieving accomplishment. If I have shared with young peachers the growing insight that some of the things that were happening to them were really being done by them under disguise, I have also known a preacher who never discovered that the voices he heard were really the voice of his repressed self. In each case the real problems had their roots farther back than the present manifestations of them.

It is with the deepest sympathy that I have listened to these people as they told me in direct and indirect ways not to look too deeply into their religious life. Their fears that psychotherapy would destroy their faith were genuine. Because they could not untangle the mixture of faith and neurosis in their mental processes, they could not be sure that anyone could do so. They feared lest that they must keep all to keep anything. What a relief such people have experienced when they discovered that it is possible to pluck up the tares and leave the wheat to thrive in the new, purified environment.

Summary

Personality is a unit, and whatever affects one part of it affects all of it. When a problem of choice between alternatives is such that it cannot be readily settled, there results strain within the personality. Such a choice may well involve not only a decision between the outward pressures which move a person in opposite directions, but between inner values. In that case, the choice is between two possible selves. If this becomes too difficult a choice to resolve consciously, it may well be repressed. Repression is a process of pushing material out of consciousness. It is not a deliberate or conscious process, and the individual is therefore neither aware of the repression nor of the material that has been repressed. Since the conflict has been removed from consciousness, but not from the personality, the effects of it continue to affect the entire personality. James expresses this concept when he says, *"A double minded man is unstable in all his ways"* (1:8).

4

ANXIETY – CONFLICT AND TENSION IN MODERN LIFE

The demanding nature of the Christian religion and the pluralistic society in which we live give us a great number of possible sources of inner conflicts that are not easily resolved. It often seems that no matter how one decides some questions, he cannot help but lose. If a person does not have enough resources to bear up under the consequences of his choices, then he tends to repress the problems. They are swept under the rug, but they leave lumps. How to achieve the necessary resources is in part the subject of chapters seven and eight. Here we are concerned with the nature of these conflicts, with what really happens when we try to ignore rather than settle them, and with the persistent and strange ways they have of living on in our personalities.

First let us see what kinds of problems typically lead to a double-mindedness that leads to anxiety that leads to illness.

Some Sources of Anxiety

The following list of sources of ambivalence in our culture is borrowed from a standard textbook in the psychology of the abnormal.[1] It does not include those early childhood

---

[1]James C. Coleman, *Abnormal Psychology and Modern Life, Second Edition* (Chicago: Scott Foresman and Co., 1956).

sources which were mentioned, but not discussed, at the end of the previous chapter.

1. Many people have a real struggle with their relationship to their parents. They feel they ought to love them, but it is very hard to do so. The truth of the matter may be that these parents are really very difficult people, even though they are church members, or even ministers.

I doubt that there is anyone so impossible for a child to live with as the minister father who "knows all the answers." Such a man has very little of the humility about which he preaches. He is far from gracious and kind. He is probably a man who solves his own problems by denying that they exist, even though his family can see them quite clearly. This puts the child into an impossible position. To accept the truth which father preaches requires him to reject the father, for father is a living denial of much that he preaches.

The father doesn't need to be a preacher, you understand, in order for him to deny by his life what he preaches with his lips. Whatever the conflict, there are many children who cannot stand up under the consequences of rejecting such a parent — you can imagine what the consequences could be! Neither can they accept the parent. So the child is trapped into using the parent's method out of the situation: he sweeps the problem under the rug by way of repression, and declares that his parents are paragons of virtue, and home is an ocean of love. The child may well believe this, but it is no wonder his thinking can become confused.

In chapter 3, several instances were given of people who seemed to have a religious problem, but for whom the more basic problem lay in their relationships with their families. These people were creating a religious problem as a cover-up for something that seemed greater to them — their horrible and contradictory impulses toward their parents.

Wayne Oates, in an effective analogy, says that a religious problem is frequently only the "showcase for the warehouse of parent-child conflicts."[2] Imagine how great must be the conflict when a person would rather doubt the existence of God than to think about the real issue!

2.   Another of the sources of conflict that cause people to be "unstable in all their ways" is that of honesty versus personal advantage. If you have ever tried to sell a product, or to advertise one, you will know the internal pulls which can work on a person who has any conscience at all. How about the opportunity to cheat in school? The great problem is not whether one will get caught, but the inner battle between two possible selves. Or, take the preacher who is trying hard to persuade a resistant audience of a point on which he is not very sure but in which he has invested considerable emotional interest. The speaker who wants desperately to drive home what is, to him, an important point, is under great pressure at times. In the past few years my wife and I have noted with alarm that several very ancient stories have showed up in the mouths of a number of preachers, each of whom told it as having happened to him personally. The conflict of personal advantage versus honesty is a real conflict for most of us, including preachers.

James observed this conflict of personal advantage versus integrity in his Christian friends. He says, *"For instance, two visitors may enter your place of worship, one a well-dressed man with gold rings, and the other a poor man in shabby clothes. Suppose you pay special attention to the well-dressed man and say to him, 'Please take this seat', while to the poor*

[2]Oates, *op. cit.,* p. 78.

*man you say, 'You can stand; or you may sit here on the floor
by my footstool', do you not see that you are inconsistent and
judge by false standards?"* (2:2-4, NEB).

3. There is often a conflict of dependence versus independence. We are taught to be self-reliant, courageous, able
to "stand on our own feet"; but as soon as one tries to do this
he finds there are many things against it. People do not like
someone who is different from them. We find that if we are
going to be independent we also have to bear the consequences
of our actions without recourse to others. To be free from
control also means that we are free from protection. To be
free from parents we must also be able to pay the bill and
carry the work load. How many of us hesitate on the brink of
decision in such matters? How we wish we could be free, yet
how we want to have the advantages of childhood! How we
wish to forge ahead to new heights, but how we want the
sheltering fold of the church, or other fellowship, which may
be unwilling to move forward.

I remember a college professor who wanted very much to
be the head of a department, but who desperately needed the
emotional support of others. He made himself helpless in order
that others would fight his battles for him but in doing so he
also lost his leadership. In the end he had nothing left but his
ambivalence, and moved to another location, where he doubtless repeated the pattern.

The overprotected person will probably never be able to
venture forth, and will probably always hate himself for his
weakness. He may always hate the fact that his wife makes
his decisions for him, but he "loves" her too much (and needs
her too much) to be able to make the decisions for himself.

The conflict of dependence versus freedom is the subject
of Erich Fromm's justly famous trilogy of books, *Escape From*

Freedom, Man For Himself, and *The Sane Society.* They are good reading, and will do much to explain why dictators have such an appeal to so many people. The Christian Church has always had a great many of such dictators, who offer their followers the security of needing to make no decisions. Those who follow them are the crawling slaves of un-Christlike men, but they are saved the anxiety that can come from the responsibilities involved in the freedom of choosing their own beliefs. It is safe to predict that for the foreseeable future the church will have large masses of members who want such dictators.

4. Another conflict in our times is that of fear versus positive action. We need realistic fear to protect ourselves from danger, but we also need courage in danger. Throughout childhood we are taught both to fear and to be courageous. Because we think fear is always bad, Coleman says, "Many people expend their efforts fighting the *feeling* of fear and trying to conceal it rather than learning to function effectively in spite of it."[3] We are afraid to admit that we are afraid.

It is taken for an evidence of the Christian life that we shall exhibit something which is given the biblical phrase, "peace that passeth understanding." This, however, is too frequently preached by ministers who spend the greater part of their sermons in whipping their audiences into a frenzy of fear. It is also too often the testimony of frenzied people, who are really afraid not to have the "peace that passeth understanding." They tend to give very insistent testimonies which are denied by the very insistence of their testimony.

We are easily caught between the feeling that we should be afraid and the feeling that we should do something about the

---

[3]Coleman, *op. cit.,* p. 138.

situation. Thus we wind up fighting the fear rather than the things of which we are afraid.

A simple and oft-repeated expression of the conflict between fear and positive action is that of the girl who finds a spider crawling up her leg, and begins to jump up and down and scream, "A tarantula! A tarantula!" A more realistic person may say to her, "Well brush it off." To which our panic-stricken girl replies, "I can't bear to touch it!" She is, of course, trying to shake it off by her jumping.

Assuming that it really is a tarantula, and that there is some reality to her fears, we still cannot understand why she cannot take the most direct course of positive action and whisk it off. Her statement that she can't bear to touch it is only partly correct, because she *is* touching it — it is on her leg. The statement must be interpreted to mean that her need not to interfere with her fear is the important fact.

For anyone who hasn't had this feeling or experience, such an irresolution is not easily understandable. Most of us react to fear in a swift and automatic way. For us who stand calmly on the side of this case, it soon becomes evident that something is going on which does not appear in what we see. There must be some reason aside from the facts of the situation which make it necessary for the girl to avoid the reasonable solution. Thus, we are led to look for deeper conflict still — fear versus action — which uses this incident as a characteristic expression of her personality.

5. Then there is the struggle between avoiding reality and facing reality. The person who has made a bad marriage is tempted to push the matter out of his mind. By overlooking some things, he hopes that this will keep matters from getting impossible.

There are those who have had what they consider to be

valid religious experiences or beliefs, which, according to some formula, are supposed to free them from their former nature. If these people are not as much changed as the formula says they should be, it is very hard to face that truth. The fact of the matter is that they *do* still get angry, and they *do* still have evil desires, even though the doctrine says they should not have; and this is very hard to face.

James particularly tries to get his readers to face the uncertainties of life and the certainty of death. *"You have no idea what tomorrow may bring,"* he says. *"Your life, what is it? You are no more than a mist, seen for a little while and then dispersing. What you ought to say is: 'If it be the Lord's will, we shall live to do this or that.' But instead, you boast and brag, and all such boasting is wrong. Well then, the man who knows the good he ought to do and does not do it is a sinner"* (4:14-17, NEB).

"The good he ought to do" is not merely a general reference to all kinds of good, as it is often quoted, but a specific admonition to face life realistically. James has no use for people who cover up the uncertainties of life by pretending that everything is just all right and everything will work out according to plan. He calls this attitude sin. The psychologist calls it unrealistic, but notes that it may be either a cause or a result of mental illness. Be it sickness or sin, the results are undesirable.

There are so many facts about one's self to which a person would like to close his eyes in hopes that they will go away. One seems to feel, "If I am really like that, I cannot bear myself. On the other hand, if I don't admit the truth about myself I'm a liar. What shall I do? Can I face the facts?"

Does a person dare to say, "But I *am* a big self-pitying baby. I *am* inadequate for the job. I *am* sexually attracted to the wrong people. I *do* get very angry, even when I try not to show it. I *have* made the wrong decision. I just *don't* measure up to what I thought I was. Everybody else seems to understand this, and I know that I should, but I just *don't*. I'm supposed to have a 'glorious experience,' a 'glowing testimony,' and a 'love for souls,' but I just *don't*"? Does one dare to admit to himself that, "As important as all these things may be, they just aren't true of me"? That takes more courage than many people can muster. It is easier to pretend a little, stretch the point, overlook a few things, and hope that everything will be all right.

How many counselors can multiply cases such as the man who said to me, "I didn't realize I was falling in love until it was too late." Others seemed to see what was happening, but he did not. There is no reason to believe that he was consciously untruthful. The conflict between "want" and "ought" was so great it could not be faced consciously. One suspects that in every case of this kind there must be even more repressed problems in the background. The first question one is tempted to ask is, "How does he really feel toward his wife? Is he partly unconscious of his feelings here also?"

It is easier to say, "There really is no problem. It would only make matters worse to face it. After all, I can go on indefinitely without anyone finding out, so why not go on? Let's cross the bridge when we get there." The trouble for such a person is that this is not a way out at all, and he is not at peace with such double-mindedness. He cannot live in a make-believe world and in a real world at the same time. He cannot hold on to error and hope to reap truth. He cannot be both of these antagonistic persons at once. The problem which he cannot face consciously becomes the source of endless unconscious anxiety, and anxiety is the raw material of neurotic behavior.

Whereas the theologian would quite appropriately dwell on sin at this point, the psychologist uses the word "sickness." I think James will show us that the results, by whatever name, are so very similar that the distinctions between sickness and sin become rather vague.

A short-term case took place at the rear door of a small country church. A middle-aged unmarried man lingered until others had left. Most pastors and other public speakers are familiar with this approach. It is the way of a person who has a deep problem, and doesn't trust other people with the information. It is also the way of a person who wants the pastor all to himself. This kind of person usually has a feeling that he has so much to say that it cannot be inserted in the rather brief casual comments that people make as they leave the meeting.

This man was as skillful at deceiving speakers as he was at deceiving himself. He approached me by saying that he had a question which no one had been able to answer. He then listed a number of nationally prominent persons for whom I have great respect, and said that each of them had failed. He further flattered me by saying that they had all given him the old clichés, but they did not seem to understand the problem. He thought I was the person who could give him the answer.

I must confess that my first natural bloom of omniscient feeling faded as I reflected on the impressive list of my superiors who had failed to untie this Gordian knot, and I began to feel a little frightened. No doubt I was feeling the full force of what he was unconsciously saying beneath the surface of flattery: "I have a problem that nobody can solve. You can't solve it either. How am I expected to know the answer when the best people in America have not known it?"

And there was a second implication in that unconscious communication as well, to the effect that, "I want you to reassure me that I can go on living with my unanswerable problem, because I don't want to have it solved."

Since he talked at considerable length there was time for me to regain my senses and regroup my resources so that I could take my attention off my own panic (for he had accurately hit me at a vulnerable spot) and turn it on his problem. It was evident that he did not want an answer but reassurance.

Finally came the question, stated in a subtly triumphant manner which indicated how unanswerable he regarded it, and how confident he was that I would leave him with the problem unresolved: "What is sin?"

I tried to put him off by saying the Bible had answers to that question. He countered by saying he had read the Bible and it gave him no help. So, with the courage of desperation (for it is always a somewhat breathless experience to throw open the back door of a person's guarded secret self) I said, "I think you are quite right. I believe these people whom you have mentioned could not answer your question. Neither can I. But I'm sure you can. I think you know what sin is, and you rather wish you didn't."

His manner and tone changed. The conversation had ended. He said somewhat reflectively, "Yes, I do know what sin is." And I left him with some comment to the effect that I hoped he would be able to work effectively on the basis of his insight. I was satisfied, and so was he, and we each went home. A short case.

What was sin for him? I don't know, and it doesn't matter. After that encounter with himself *he* knew, and that does matter. I was in the community for one evening and have never been back. If there had been opportunity, this man should have followed through his first insight with extended therapy, but there was no other opportunity, and something basic had been gained. The true source of his problem had now in some new way become conscious. It could now be dealt with directly. I hope it was.

The Nature of Anxiety

When such conflicts as we have illustrated are not readily resolved, they exist in a state of tension that we have called ambivalence. Ambivalence easily creates a state of anxiety. When a person finds the conflict so great that it must be pushed out of consciousness, this inadequacy to deal with the problem is anxiety-producing. Let us see a bit more clearly what is the nature of anxiety, so that we can better understand the results in the personality.

Anxiety differs from fear in several ways. The source of anxiety is unconscious, and is usually within one's self; whereas fear is directed toward things one consciously knows about, and which are usually outside one's self. If I am afraid of a dog, I know it, and I know that I can avoid both the dog and the fear by walking another way. Or, if I cannot avoid the danger, at least I know what will happen to me, and I can try to rally my resources to bear up under the pain. Dreadful as fear is, at least it deals with the known.

Anxiety generally deals with hidden problems inside the person. Since one cannot bring them to consciousness, he does not know what is the source of his anxiety, and therefore he does not know what to do about it. It is characteristic of anxiety that it arises for reasons a person does not understand, because it arises from repressed problems. These are problems which were swept out of consciousness, but which are still in the personality, and which have this way of expressing themselves.

Thus it is that a person may say, "I'm all tense!" His friend says, "What are you tense about?" He replies, "I don't know. I'm just tense." "Don't be ridiculous," says his friend, "one doesn't get tense about nothing." But one *does* get tense about nothing — that is, nothing which one can identify. (It usually doesn't stay that vague, as we shall see later.)

Suppose the friend then begins to probe, and says, "What sin have you committed? Why don't you confess to the Lord?" The mention of sin and confession in this manner are likely to work in a direction opposite to that intended. That horrible thing which is already so sinful and painful that it cannot be brought to consciousness is all the less likely to come out in the presence of someone who stands ready to accuse and condemn.

It is as though the unconscious part of the mind were saying, "How could I expose myself to you? You, who stand for good and truth and blazing righteousness? I, who am confused, who am wrong no matter how I decide? No, thank you, I'll just keep things down here in the cellar of the mind where you won't see them and add your condemnation to that which I have already found too heavy to bear. Why, you would probably think my problem is very silly." At that point we leave our anxious unconscious in its soliloquy — noticing, however, that it has already begun to change the nature of the problem in the last sentence. It usually manages to change it sufficiently so that it can come out in disguised form. The sinner may even confess a sin — but not the one that is really the trouble. He just thinks it's the real trouble. Our anxious person, you see, cannot tell what is wrong. He is consciously honest. He doesn't know what is wrong himself.

If anyone thinks this state of affairs is disturbing, he is quite right. James says that a double-minded man, unstable in all his ways, is a person who is "*driven with the wind and tossed*" (1:6). In an interesting parallel to this statement by James, Freud says, "Neurotics who are compelled to reproduce this conflict (put forth) . . . the most prodigious psychic efforts on their part."[4]

If you will remember what I said earlier about the nature of tension in the body, you will see that such a person may well be exerting great physical effort because of the opposing pull of the muscles themselves, besides the emotional disturbance which he experiences. The conflict does not remain in one area of the personality. It becomes the disturbance of the entire person — body, soul and spirit.

Some Neurotic Reactions

Such a disturbance is an intolerable state of affairs. The person is all worked up about what seems to be nothing. He is tired without having worked. He is afraid when there is nothing observable of which to be afraid. He is confused in his thinking. In psychological language, he has free-floating anxiety which pervades his whole personality.

This anxiety has a way of bubbling up seemingly from nowhere, upsetting the person, and then vanishing into the void from which it came. Eventually, however, there is likely to grow up some method by which the mind seeks to ward off the anxiety. These methods have a way of turning the unknown problem into something more conscious. We call this a neurosis. There are several general types of neurotic symptoms, and within each there are innumerable variations and combinations. The symptoms are not the person's real prob-

---

[4]Freud, *op. cit.*, p. 858.

lem. They are always a way of changing the real, underlying problem into something that seems easier to deal with. The names of these kinds of neurotic transformations are not so important as an understanding of the general kinds of reactions that occur.

1. One of the ways of dealing with those unresolved tensions is to get away from them by way of tiredness and sleep. It is as though the person just gives up. He loses energy and strength of will, and just gets weak and listless. (Please notice that some people sleep more than others for the same reason that some people have longer noses than others — they were just made that way. Others lack vitamins, or have some other physical ailment or need. But this leaves us with a certain number of people who sleep more and more as their emotional problems become greater.) Unfortunately, such people are likely to wake up almost as tired as they went to bed, because the unconscious mind does not sleep when the conscious mind does. They have to go on living in their inner world even though they are asleep. Their trouble is really in that inner, unconscious world from which sleep offers no escape. This is a very self-defeating state of affairs, as all neuroses are.

2. It would be so much more convenient if the problem came out where one could see it, but of course one would rather not have his real problem become conscious, so we have this vicious cycle. For many neurotics the problem is transformed into a vague general fear that he is sick, or that something terrible is happening somewhere in the body. Physicians' offices are full of people with these general complaints. The physicians usually know that these people will continue to seek help no matter what they are told. If the physician tells them the truth — "There is nothing *physically* wrong with you" — such people only become angry and go to another

physician, and to another, and to another until someone prescribes a pill.

These people don't want to be told that their physical complaint is only a "cover up" for their real trouble. And to tell them that there is *nothing wrong* with them is not the truth. There is a great deal wrong with them. They would rather have it be a physical problem, and they appreciate the physician who agrees with them. They want to be able to say, "See, the doctor says I am sick!" The only trouble is that even then they do not get well.

The faith healing lines are full of these people. They even try to deceive the Lord (if deceive is not too strong a word for something a person doesn't know he is doing). The healer rather easily heals them of their symptoms and they go home in the high hope that now everything will be all right — and it is for a while. At the next healing meeting, however, they are likely to be in line again with some other ailment. The cause has not been cured, and that hidden cause can continue to produce these feelings of illness as long as it remains.

3. For that matter, the same is true of this next group of neurotics. These do not have just vague feelings that they are sick somewhere, but they produce very specific symptoms, for which no one can ever find an actual physical damage. For instance, such a person can very convincingly develop all the symptoms of appendicitis, even though the appendix is healthy, or probably has already been removed. Coleman tells of a patient who had been operated on for appendicitis so often that one surgeon finally tatooed on the patient's abdomen the words, "No appendix there."

I have had several patients who stated at the outset that they had heart trouble. They had been to physicians, who gave them some medication, but who also indicated that there didn't seem to be anything significantly wrong with the heart. The patients, in telling me these things, gave the feeling that the physician had given them medication pretty much as a precaution against anything he might have missed, and as a concession to their evident distress.

One of these discovered after a while that before each session the heart "acted up" just before she arrived at my office and continued until the therapy session had begun. It was thus possible to begin an exploration of the hidden meaning and use of the "heart trouble" in the neurotic pattern. So we began to discover that the symptoms — which to this person were very distressing — were really a disguised way of expressing the inner anxiety. In this case we might note that the patient was a woman who, though she had a family of her own, had also stated that she was uneasy in the presence of men. If the lay reader wishes to make deductions about what was going on, he may do so, and he will likely be at least partly correct. I should warn, however, that there were other layers under this one which contained some surprising twists in the road. The symptom was a very effective decoy.

These symptoms may be so accurate that they deceive even the physician until he gets at what should be the diseased part of the body and finds the tissue in good condition. There is hardly an ailment in the medical textbooks which cannot be, and has not been, simulated in this manner. Paralysis, blindness, deafness, all manner of internal disorders, loss of sensitivity at various places in the body, and a host of other ailments can appear without any evident physical cause. To the person who says, "They are all in your head," the experienced clinician says, "You are unfortunately right, but remember that the head is the hardest part to operate on." It does not simplify the matter in the least to say it is in the head.

4. There is another whole host of reactions to internal stress which takes the form of removing one's self from the problem by way of the loss of memory. Under sufficient stress a person may lose his memory completely; or may even find himself somewhere in a strange place with no idea of who he is or how he got there. In a somewhat related neurotic reaction, he may operate as though he were two people. Although this is not very common, an authentic case is well reported in the popular book, *Three Faces of Eve.* Eve has more recently been reported to have developed a fourth face. We must not get the idea that such a multiple personality (not a split personality, please) is really multiple. It is still a unified personality which is trying to act as more than one. The results are surprising, but the part that appears to the public is only a part of the true personality. One might call it an acting out of the inner struggle.

Before we continue too far in this recital, we must point out that neurotic reactions do not occur only as a result of unresolved internal conflict. They can also occur in response to some other stresses which are able to cause anxiety. The reason we speak here of neurotic reactions is not that unresolved conflict is the only cause, but because it is often a cause. Do not make the mistake of labeling every neurotic symptom as the result of double-mindedness. Above all, remember that this book is not intended to give its readers competence as psychological diagnosticians. It cannot do that, and to try to use it that way is to court serious danger. We are engaged in a sufficient discussion of neurosis to help the reader appreciate the meanings which seem to underlie the comments of James. That is very much worth doing, even though it does not make a person a psychotherapist, nor (from a study of a part of one book of the Bible) a Bible scholar.

5. The phobic reactions are interesting manifestations of anxiety, and they, too, can be caused by unresolved double-mindedness. A phobia is an irrational fear — that is, a fear that doesn't make sense. It may be a horrible fear of doorknobs, or of small rooms, or of open places, or of almost anything.

When one goes into the history of these cases, one finds that there is nothing which should have produced such a strong reaction. In fact a phobia is a displaced anxiety, like the other neurotic symptoms. The real thing of which the person is afraid is too terrible even to think of, and the unconscious protects itself by attaching the fear to something other than the real cause. A phobia is another deflection or decoy, set up so that the conscious mind has something to focus on whenever the anxiety becomes too great, and does not need to focus on the underlying problem. It works surprisingly well for some people. There is also sometimes a secondary advantage to the phobic person, because it may get a lot of desirable attention or sympathy.

I have known a college student who left school because the fear of small places made it impossible for him to live in a college dormitory room. This kind of fear is different from a learned fear, and is quite irrational. One need only ask, "How did this student get along at home, where the rooms were no larger," to see how irrational it is. Obviously small rooms were not so much of a real problem as a displaced problem.

If a person has once been buried in a landslide, a fear of closed places is understandable. One can also teach such a person not to fear closed places when the danger is past. It takes careful methods, but it can be done. Direct methods of eliminating a phobia, however, can succeed only if the person can substitute some other neurotic symptom for the phobia, and that isn't much of a success. The phobic needs something to fear. People have been known to risk death rather than to touch the thing toward which they have a phobia. Such a reaction is not to be taken lightly. These people are in serious trouble.

6. The list is fairly complete if we mention the obsessive-compulsive reactions which take control of the conscious mind so that it cannot rid itself of undesirable thoughts or causes the person to perform meaningless and often distasteful acts for reasons which the individual cannot understand. These acts often have considerable symbolic meaning. Having mentioned them here, we leave a further discussion of them to chapter six, where they fit into a specific statement of James.

The Emotional Strain

How appropriate to this discussion is the lament of the prophet Isaiah over Israel: "Why should ye be stricken any more? . . . the whole head is sick, and the whole heart faint" (Isaiah 1:5). A person who is unable to face his emotional battles, who is driven one way and lured another, who knows that no matter how he decides he will still lose, or regardless of how he chooses he will have to give up a part of himself — such a person is hardly to be dealt with harshly. He is rather a person for whom one should have profound sympathy. As we have seen, James says of him, "*he who doubts is like a wave of the sea that is driven and tossed by the wind*" (1:6, RSV), and "*he is double-minded, and never can keep a steady course*" (1:8, NEB).

How wonderful it would be for such a person to have faith, for to have that faith would set him on a steady course. It would make up his mind. It would settle his problem. It is not for nothing that the Apostle John says, "This is the victory that overcometh the world, even our faith" (I John 5:4). Faith does not give the victory, as some people understand that statement. It *is* the victory. Once a person has the right relationship to God, the battle is over.

The question still remains, however, "How shall the weak brother get that faith?" We cannot ignore real sin, for it must be dealt with, but there are many who are ready to condemn sin, and few who are ready or able to help the sinner. This book is an attempt to give a sound basis, such as James seems to intend, upon which one can help the sinner without ignoring the sin.

Let us not be quick to condemn the neurotic. He is not only hard to live with. In the most literal sense he is having a terrible time living with himself.

Can you sympathetically imagine how horrible must be the problems within a person that would cause him rather to suffer bodily pain, bear the reproaches of others, and go through the kind of self-tortures which I have mentioned, rather than face that unknown inner problem? If you can, then you may realize that although the epistle of James has a hard and practical ring, it is really the gentle firmness of the surgeon who refuses to close his eyes to the inner malignancy and wields the cruel knife with precision to save life and to heal.

Can you understand how much such a person needs help? Then perhaps you can also understand why Jesus wept over the self-destroying Jerusalem, rather than condemning it. Is not such a person as we have described already punishing himself far more than he should? Isn't the message for such a person the message of the Christ who is presented by John as saying, "Behold, I stand at the door and knock; if any one hears my voice and opens the door, I will come in to him and eat with him, and he with me" (Revelation 3:20, RSV)?

Long experience prompts me to plead with the reader. Can

you overcome your own selfish impulses to add another blow to such a person's already heavy burden? Can the love of Christ work through you for such a person? If so, James has a task for you later in his epistle.

If, as you read these chapters, you find that they describe your own symptoms, can you take renewed courage and face your problems for what they really are? Well, perhaps not yet; it is too much to expect at this stage. The channels by which God's grace can heal the cause of these symptoms is found later in the epistle. James does indeed say that God will give insight and healing, but he does not indicate that it is either as automatic or as easy as some superficial readers of the Bible have wanted to believe.

Summary

This chapter has brought some more psychoanalytic insights to bear on what appears to have been the intention of James in his discussion of double-mindedness. Their appropriateness will become more apparent in succeeding chapters.

Some common sources of inner conflict were listed. We pointed out that when such conflicts are too difficult to resolve and are therefore pushed out of consciousness, they may be the cause of anxiety. Anxiety is related to unknown causes, which are usually found within the personality itself, as compared with the fear of known dangers outside our selves. Anxiety, in turn, tends to work itself out in ways which disguise the original cause of the anxiety, and to manifest itself in symptoms which are called neurotic reactions. There are several kinds of neurotic behavior and we listed some of them. Since the causes of all symptoms are essentially the same, the fact that James appears later to deal with several symptoms specifically would justify the conclusion that he offers insight into all neurotic behavior, to a greater or lesser extent. Having shown that

such a displacement of the real problem into a neurotic symptom may well cause the person to live under the enormous
emotional strain which James calls *"driven with the wind and
tossed,"* we are ready to consider two specific examples of
neurotic behavior which are mentioned by James as being
directly related to double-mindedness.

5

AGGRESSION—INNER AND OUTER WARS

Inner conflicts continue to produce symptoms within the personality even though they seem to have been forgotten. And all too often they do not stay within the personality, but spill over onto other people — as I am sure we have discovered from personal experience. When that happens there is usually war! Here we shall explore why and how such personal inner conflicts are transformed into conflicts between people.

Causes of Aggression

There are a great number of reasons why individuals and nations are hostile and aggressive toward one another. Each discipline has some valid answers of its own, which doubtless fit into the total picture. The sociologist speaks of social forces and intolerable living conditions; the economist points to poverty and economic imperialism; the historian points to crucial events and key leaders (these statements are, of course, oversimplifications of their valuable contributions). In chapter 4:1-7, James says that the trouble lies inside each individual. That is an answer which is dear to the psychologist's heart.

The psychologist recognizes at least two inner sources of aggression. The first comes from the basic animal response to any kind of frustration. When the infant does not get what he wants, he goes into a rage and responds with violence that is entirely unconcerned about what happens to anyone else. He may even injure himself in his indiscriminate lashing out at whatever is near. Society has erected all kinds of prohibitions and restrictions against the direct expression of such natural aggressiveness, and quite practical considerations tend to inhibit them as well. The psychologist calls this reaction libidinal aggression.

It is interesting to find that studies of juvenile delinquents have several times shown that they are less troubled with anxiety and mental illness than average, normally behaved young persons. They don't worry about their aggressive impulses and don't try to control them. They just let them out, like infants. There is no great amount of internal conflict because the delinquent usually decides what to do about his anger (if following an impulse can be called a decision) and proceeds to act upon it. Since he usually has a weak conscience, the violent behavior tends to work off the inner tension and so he has a period of relief. The results are socially disastrous, but they are not likely to cause the delinquent to have mental illness of the sort we are discussing.

Sooner or later someone makes the comment to almost every male psychotherapist, "How is it that most of your patients seem to be women?" In many instances this is a false observation, but there is some truth to the impression that more women than men come for therapy. One of the important reasons is that men are more likely to get their "treatment" in jail. That is, they are less likely to hold in their impulses, and so they are more likely to commit crimes which get them in trouble with the law. Also, when they are neurotic, they are more likely to take out their anxiety in the form of action against others than are women. Thus, both they and society are less likely to regard themselves as mentally ill, and they are less likely to find themselves in psychotherapy.

Most criminals are not mentally ill, but some are. Unfortunately, though these persons probably deserve to be punished, yet punishment often only gives them a further excuse for acting out their hostilities and avoiding their real inner problems. Having worked for a while on the staff of a clinic in a correctional institution, I am pleased to note that new attitudes toward crime are responsible for an increasing emphasis on giving such people the help they need with those inner problems.

The second cause of aggressive behavior goes under the name of "displaced aggression." This means that the person is severely blocked in his desires, but cannot attack the real source of his frustrations, so he attacks something else. This transfer to something else is usually unconscious, although people are sometimes at least partly aware of it. The more serious the original, repressed problem, the less likely it is that the displacement of aggression will be a conscious process. So we see that it works by the same process as other neurotic reactions. The reason it is discussed separately is that James points it out for special treatment in chapter four.

This sort of aggression can come about as the result of unresolved internal conflict, just as James says it did for his Christian readers (4:2). The fact is that Christians have very high standards of conduct, and these easily produce more internal conflicts than are experienced by others.

We have already seen that emotions which are bottled up tend to come out at other places, and that the second possibility is often worse than the first. Therefore, it is important to know that the aggressive impulses, which are a part of the normal human equipment for survival, can be turned to creative ends.

Fortunately, most of us make use of them creatively most of the time.

Frustration is inevitable in human existence. It is, indeed, desirable in manageable quantities. Without some kind of frustration it is likely that no modern learning, civilization or art would have developed. It seems that man would be pretty much of a vegetable if the circumstances did not make him hungry, dissatisfied with the plumbing, yearning for the security of more knowledge or better political institutions, and in every other way reaching out toward better solutions for the circumstances which frustrate him at the moment.

Thus we see that frustration can lead to aggressive behavior which is constructive, creative, artistic, and in keeping with the principles of loving human interaction. That is, if we have learned how to use those channels effectively. Sports, hard work, creativity are all excellent channels for the aggressive drives of people who know how to use them. There is a seriously mistaken notion abroad that psychoanalysis—and Freud in particular — have advocated a complete abandonment to the rule of our impulses. Nothing could be farther from the truth. Freud pointed out that the greatest service a civilization can render is to provide useful ways of redirecting those impulses for the common good of all. He called this sublimation — that is, a sublime transformation of the potentially destructive human motives into useful ends.

When discussing this in a class, one young woman said that whenever she became quite motivated in a manner that seemed to demand an angry expression, she started to clean the house. As she told about it, we could see the pots and pans rattling, the dust flying, and the furniture clattering out of her way — but the end result was both a release of the drive, and a satisfyingly clean house.

Of course, the young men who play football are always told it is a way of displacing their aggression. Sometimes they don't like to hear that, but I have known some who are quite aware of it, who grin and point out that football works only when that aggression is kept within certain controls. There are rules which prevent indiscriminate destruction, and there are intellectual demands upon the player which require that his rational intellect, rather than his raw impulse, direct his activity; otherwise he executes a poor play, and the coach puts him on the bench.

One of the best places to watch the play of emotions in creativity is in the nursery school, where children from the ages of three to six are given opportunty to do finger painting, or other similar forms of art. Any nursery school teacher can give you many illustrations of how the emotions come out on that paper. I have seen a little boy begin a beautiful finger painting, then seem to get sucked into it, as his eyes became glazed and his hands reduced the sheet to a total ugly blur. I have seen this same boy make the paper sparkle with sunlight and laughter. It may be that this boy will for the rest of his life find some expression for his inner feelings in painting — whether he becomes a professional painter or not.

Unfortunately, not all of us have discovered what channels of release and creative expression work for us personally, nor have we learned to use well those channels we have discovered. So there is a tendency for our anger not to be *transformed* into better goals and methods, but merely *displaced* onto other objects.

James points out that he is speaking about this kind of displaced aggression, which arises out of a mind in conflict. *"You want something which you cannot have and so you are bent on murder"* (4:2, NEB). For the other kind, which is sometimes called psychopathic behavior one must turn elsewhere in the Bible, notably the epistles of Peter and parts of the Old Testament.

It is impossible to make a physical attack on something that is as non-physical as an internal conflict. However, the person with an internal conflict is under great strain, and is severely blocked in his attempt at a satisfactory solution. (Such a blocking of a goal is called a "frustration.") The degree of the inner tension and of its resultant disorganization of the personality is indicated by James in the now oft-repeated statement, *"driven with the wind and tossed."* Clinically we see it as severe, recurrent headaches, grossly disorganized behavior, or the variety of illnesses which were mentioned in the previous chapter.

It is quite understandable that such a person, who dares not face his problem, must turn somewhere else to release his tension. He often does this by becoming extremely hostile toward someone who cannot very well defend himself, and who is entirely unrelated to the original conflict.

In this manner people engage in what is called "scapegoating." They get unreasonably angry at someone who is not at all at fault, but whom they can blame because they can get away with it. The term, of course, comes from the Old Testament practice of putting the sins symbolically on a goat (which could hardly have been guilty) and banishing it into the desert. In the same way scapegoating takes place today, with the scapegoat being perhaps one's husband or wife, parents, the Jews, the Negroes, or perhaps the Russians or the Americans. Bad as some of them are, the Russians are also being used as a way of venting anger quite apart from any evil they may have done or intended. This is easy to do since when one is angry it is always socially quite respectable to verbally kick the communists. In some other countries Americans serve the same irrational ends.

Displacement of anger is not only from the real cause within a man to a more convenient person; it is also a displacement of guilt from the real cause within himself to someone else whom he can consciously blame. Thus it is that the person who does the scapegoating does not see himself as irritable or fussy or cruel. He believes that he has discovered the person who is doing wrong, and therefore he considers himself to be engaged in righteous indignation and in proper punishment of such a person. The scapegoater then proceeds to abuse the husband, wife, child, Negroes, Jews, or the cat, with the same intensity as he unconsciously feels his own guilt deserves.

Logic has no effect upon the scapegoater, for if it did, he would not have started scapegoating in the first place. Furthermore, if he were to allow himself to discover that he is punishing an innocent person, the guilt which he has tried to push off on that person would come back upon himself with redoubled force.

The germ of truth in his accusations, and the conviction that he has found a righteous cause which deserves the great emotion he has ready to spend combine to make the scapegoater a rather vehement person. Recently, in talking to a group about this subject, a person interrupted the lecture to insist hotly that one of the illustrations I had used was indeed a righteous cause, and not an illustration of scapegoating. This person's willingness to break the commonly accepted rules for the conduct of a lecture, his picking out a very small and specific part of the lecture, and the blunt, harsh insistence with which he drove home his convictions were rather startling to those in the audience who have not become accustomed to such behavior. However, as the temperature of the emotional climate cooled down, most people present realized that they had seen an example of what I had been talking about. I hope I treated the man with the kindness which his illness deserves without denying the facts — but I leave that to my audience to judge.

It is noteworthy that in times when we are not at war, and when castigating the devil has fallen out of vogue, and when most people try to blend into the moral and ethical culture rather than take up crusading issues, a great number of church people seemingly need to join extremist groups in order to find a good scapegoating cause.

Obviously, a direct appeal to reason is far worse than useless. If it succeeds at all, the only thing it could possibly do for the scapegoater is to make him feel more internally troubled than he already is, with the result that he would need even more neurotic defenses against seeing what is already too terrible to face. The only way to help him is to find some method of washing away the original guilt-provoking conflict and leaving him clean. Because his conflict is unconscious, this is a very difficult task. How can one deal openly with a problem which cannot be brought to consciousness? Once again we have the vicious cycle. Let it be sufficient at this time to say that James was well aware of the inner sources of scapegoating. The method of healing he deals with later.

I suspect that sometimes the vehemence with which some Christians castigate the devil is not because they really know him to be so bad, but because they are afraid of how bad they are themselves. Such displacement of the conflict gives the sufferer somebody else to kick instead of himself. But, unfortunately, it does not ease the pain within him, and therefore the scapegoater is engaged in an unending battle with himself and others.

Scapegoating in Practical Situations

The awareness that inner troubles cause social conflict is expressed in the common observation which is made to a person who is irritable: "What's eating you?" The more perceptively the question is applied, the more likely it is to get a sharp reply.

So James is quite in agreement with the psychologist when he says that fightings and wars come because our desires are at war in ourselves. Whenever you find a person who constantly quarrels, you know a person who has severe inner problems which he cannot face directly. Such people differ from those who "contend earnestly for the faith" in that they are "earnestly contentious for the faith." No matter where they are or what is going on, they always find something to quarrel about. They are always crusading for or against something. Certain congregations, and even denominations, by their *manner* of emphasizing their separation from the world manage to accumulate to themselves a disproportionate number of people who need to get involved in a fight. They are rather like religious mercenaries, at the hire of anyone who has a fight.

The trouble with having such people in a group is that they can turn their battles toward their supposed friends as easily as upon the "outsiders," and they often do. The more I have known about church quarrels, some of which have resulted in the founding of new denominations, the more I have found that the basic issues were rarely doctrinal, and usually personal. Even when there was a doctrinal issue, it took certain personalities to split it into a battle; and it has been disturbingly enlightening to see just who joined the battle on each side of such an issue. There were strange bedfellows, unless one understands this chapter of James.

There are some other ways in which the inwardly unhappy

person may try to put the problem elsewhere, and they fit well into this discussion.

There is the person who takes the completely opposite position from his real problem, in an unconscious attempt to control it. This person may also be very contentious (although his device may not result in quarrelsomeness), but the difference is that instead of fighting in a general way, he points to his source of inner difficulty by being sensitive primarily to that which represents a psychological opposite of his trouble. If he feels inwardly guilty because he secretly very much desires something he thinks he should not have or do, he may take a strong public position opposite to his desire. The harder he fights his favorite sin the farther he seems to be putting himself from it, and the greater barrier he appears to be putting between himself and the feared sin — but the more it enables him to talk about it constantly.

Talk is admittedly a poor second best to the pleasure of sinning wholeheartedly, but it is the best that some of us ambivalent Christians can get. Much of the unnecessary and too-emphatic public shouting about the evils of sex, tobacco, alcohol, money, and a variety of other subjects is of this sort. The crusader who is on this kind of warpath may or may not be secretly doing what he publicly so vehemently condemns, but he is fighting an inward battle on an issue which he is not quite able to face consciously. Such a disguised, opposite reaction is called a "reaction formation." It can lead to problems of the sort I have mentioned (but it can also turn such tricks as disguising hostility with sugary sweetness).

There are people who see real dangers and react toward them with the vigor that the gravity of the threat calls for. They can be distinguished from the people who are engaging in the sort of reaction formation I have described. In part, the difference lies in the way the genuine reformer relaxes on the subject when it is not appropriate, or when the danger is not present. The "reaction former" drags the subject in by its heels at every chance, regardless of whether there is a real reason or not, and regardless of whether there is any real threat.

The real reason he brings up the subject at inopportune times is that he has only this way of handling his anxiety. This is why, for instance, a complete stranger may slash at his favorite "whipping boy" the first time he meets you, before he could possibly know on what side of the issue you might stand.

Picture such a situation. Here is a person whose internal conflict makes him feel anxious, insecure and unworthy. He would like to have your approval, as most people would, but he doesn't know you, and therefore he feels more insecure. He doesn't know how to "get on the good side of you," and his inner fearfulness makes him assume that you are probably not as friendly as he would like you to be. As his insecurity rises, he turns to the only way he has of handling his anxiety, namely, insisting that he is not the bad kind of person which he fears he is. So he proceeds to prove this by launching into his favorite subject.

Without warning or provocation you now find yourself confronted by a haughty, self-righteous, angry, dogmatic person. To be sure he may not be speaking about a subject that has any interest for you, but you are still confronted by that kind of emotional situation. Since most of us still have a little insecurity ourselves, we are prone to react to that felt hostility as though it were directed at us. (Indeed, it is directed at us, regardless of the subject of the conversation, because this is the "reaction former's" way of dealing with the anxiety he feels in our presence.) Later we may say, "Now why did I respond to him with so much emotion?"

Frequently enough a young man will sit in my office and call down righteous and physical destruction on a certain brand of evildoers. It is always a delight when one of them pauses and says, "Now why do I feel that way?" That question has the hopeful glimmer of insight which can be nurtured into healthy consideration of good and evil as they really are. When the patient has given me clues that he is able to bear such an interpretation, I am apt to say something like, "You feel very guilty about your desire to do what they are doing; and you wish for them the severe punishment which you are afraid you deserve." It is wonderful to see the kind of relaxation of the face, the hands, the whole body, even the voice, as such a person realizes his secret is understood by someone who does not minimize the guilt, but who still accepts the guilty. The truth may well be that I have no idea at that point whether or not this young man is guilty of the misdeeds he fears. I do know his *feeling* of guilt, and for the moment that is sufficient. More will follow in due time.

Another distinction between the genuine and the false reformer lies in the manner in which they handle the subject. In a reaction formation the subject is really pleasant to the crusader, but he must make it look unpleasant. Or, it may really be unpleasant, but he needs to make it look pleasant. Thus the false reformer tends to shout too loudly, insist much more than is necessary, and above all, stay with the subject far beyond the necessary amount of time. This is why one can probably get a more vivid, lurid, and sexy picture of the evils of sex from a person who is engaging in a reaction formation against sex, than from any other source. Unfortunately, church-going young people have some of their ideas about sex perverted by reaction forming preachers and confessions as well as by way of the "gutter."

Some psychologists have branded various of the prophets, as well as the Apostle Paul, as neurotics. One of the reasons for this is that the psychologists did not believe that these people were dealing with real problems. If, on the other hand, what the prophets saw was indeed reality, then their behavior with all its urgency is very normal.

There is another specific way of turning one's inner trouble into an outward fight. It has already been suggested in the discussion of scapegoating. This is to project one's inner problem onto someone else and condemn him for it. In part, this is what the "reaction former" is doing. The simplest illustration of such projection is the person who shouts, "I'm not angry! You're angry!" In the same way the thief trusts no one, and the troubled soul sees only trouble in others. By this means they find something to quarrel about. They are saying, "You are the cause of all my troubles, so I shall retaliate!" It reminds one of the goat that rushed at his image in the mirror.

In Genesis 4:6, 7, God suggests that such an inner problem of two selves was going on in Cain, the first murderer. "And the Lord said to Cain, Why art thou wroth? and why is thy countenance fallen? If thou doest well, shalt thou not be accepted? and if thou doest not well, sin lieth at the door. And unto thee shall be his desire, and thou shalt rule over him." But Cain didn't want to face the rejection of his sacrifice on the basis of his inner struggle; he rather blamed his brother and went out and killed him. John says, "And why did he murder him? Because his own deeds were evil and his brother's righteous" (I John 3:12, RSV). This is hardly a reason for murder, unless you understand the mechanisms of projection and of scapegoating.

International Conflicts

Whatever James had in mind when he said that wars are caused by these internal conflicts, he must have meant the conflict of more than two persons. He may indeed have meant the relatively small church fights which the New Testament says existed in that early church. But I propose that he had intertribal and international conflict in mind as well.

Once again we find Freud speaking on the subject, and saying that whereas ambivalence causes interpersonal conflicts, ". . . we are confident of finding a similar solution in the case of races."[1]

It is not too hard to find historical examples of countries where the internal problems spilled over into international conflict. In fact, there are authoritative conjectures that the inner problems of a Kaiser precipitated the first World War. Needless to say, the Kaiser did not fight the war alone. The frustrations of large groups of people can result in serious conflicts between groups. In effect, groups get together to blame others for their unresolved frustrations. One can see this on the playground any day of the week, with only a little perception. Eric Hoffer, in his controversial book *The True Believer*, dwells on all kinds of frustrations which he believes to have been the historical causes of mass movements of people. You will not always agree with him, but if you even disagree with most things he says this book is likely to start many new thoughts. Psychoanalyst Erich Fromm develops this mass frustration theme in his books as well.

At this point I remember the comment of the New York University sociologist, Professor Dan W. Dodson, who says that in America today most churches insist that their ministers shall preach things which the members have no serious inten-

---

[1]*Op. cit.*, p. 860.

tion of living by. If he is right about Christians, then is it any wonder that we are full of inward and outward conflicts? And is it any wonder that in looking around for someone else to blame, we are so ready to go to war with each other, or, for that matter, with some other country?

Self-Displaced Aggression

The ambivalent person hates himself for the very things he wants. If God indeed responded to his asking, and gave him what he requests, that would not bring him happiness. As James tells us, *"Ye ask amiss"* (4:3). The ambivalent person cannot enjoy God's gift because he also wants its opposite. The problem is not what he can *have*, but what he can *enjoy*, and what kind of person he must be in order to be able to enjoy God's gift. How far can such a state of inner self-defeat go? Let us see.

Gardner Murphy looks at the problem and says that, for the psychologist, the classical theory of hedonism has no meaning. Neurotic people at least do not seek pleasure and avoid pain.

> If the individual discovers that the course upon which he is embarking will bring more distress than satisfaction, the theory [of hedonism] requires that he abandon it. But he does not. The nature of human conflict involves self-defeat of the gravest sort, an extreme incapacity to be rational or to make any such calculations as the classical theory requires.[2]

His friend and colleague Karl Menninger goes even farther, and says that ambivalence is characteristic of alcoholics, and of people who commit suicide. In fact, he says that every case of suicide he has ever investigated involved severe ambivalence as an important factor.[3]

---

[2]Murphy, *op. cit.*, p. 303.
[3]Karl A. Menninger, *Man Against Himself* (New York: Harcourt, Brace and Company, 1938), pp. 42-45 and 170-177.

The dynamics of such a suicide are not too difficult to understand. The person feels that suicide is a way of resolving the unbearable conflict. He may, indeed, not know what the conflict is, but by killing himself he both ends the struggle and punishes himself for having the struggle. It is really a "self-displaced aggression." His inner pain is so great that he would like to lash out against someone, but his conscience, or the circumstances, will not let him do that, so he turns the force of the blow upon himself. He is no more the cause of the trouble than anyone else, and although he is destroying himself he is not really attacking the problem.

Before the days of tranquilizers I saw a mental patient who had to be forceably restrained because she bit chunks out of her own arm. I have also known a college student who moved in a cycle from what she considered to be a sanctification experience, to a carefully laid plan to murder her mother, to an abrupt change of plans which led her to the nearest body of water in order to commit suicide. She stopped short of that and came for help. In her case the several elements of the process are fairly clearly outlined. In another case a man sought both to get his wife's pity and to get revenge on her when he aimed a knife at his own heart. Underneath it all was a further ambivalence, for he was a cripple who both depended on his wife and hated her for his weakness.

Let us understand that man is not nearly as rational as the armchair thinker sometimes makes him out to be. At the same time, let us realize that he is understandable, and even rather predictable in his irrationality. Most important of all, let us see ourselves as clearly as we can, so that we may be spared such gross irrationalities as these, if possible. Internal conflict breeds interpersonal conflict.

A seminary friend of mine half-jokingly said he intended

to translate the Bible into Brooklynese so that his friends could understand it too. Shortly thereafter the Revised Standard Version was issued, and since then there has been a wonderful flood of translations and paraphrases. Paraphrases are sometimes useful. Let us see if a rather loose paraphrase of James 4:1-7 into psychologese will help the reader to get a clearer image of at least a part of the intention of that passage. Here it is.

1. *Do you wonder what causes all this aggressive and antisocial behavior among people who are supposed to be Christians? Well, I'll tell you. It's a problem of unresolved ambivalence. You want things which are basically in conflict with each other.* 2. *So you go to all manner of lengths, including physical violence, to get them. Your internal boiling makes your external brawling, but nothing gets you any real satisfaction, because you keep looking to the wrong sources.* [Marginal note: It might also read — *This crazy, mixed-up kid is fighting himself all over the place, and getting everybody else involved in it.*] 3. *So you go to church and pray about the matter, but that doesn't get you anywhere because you are trying to get a just, righteous God to give you things to use ·wastefully and selfishly on a confused set of conflicting desires, and God just won't be integrated into a system like that.* 4. *Now, friends, use your heads; you know you can't get away with that. You have to make up your minds. The perfectly self-controlled God and your uncontrolled desires are antithetical to each other — and you can't have your cake and eat it too.* 5. *Furthermore, there are tremendous inner forces at work in you, jealously battling for control. God doesn't give you up so easily!* 6. *The more defenses you set up, the worse the struggle becomes. The harder the selfish interest struggles for control, the more intense becomes the force of good that battles*

against it, and the more wretched you become. If you would give up the selfish side of the struggle, and integrate yourselves around what you know to be the divine side of the issue, you would find that the very forces which have fought and condemned you up to this point would become your resources for inner strength. 7. Submit yourselves, therefore unto God, and once you have made a clear decision, you will find that the other rejected forces melt away amazingly.

Jesus said that he who hates his brother in his heart has potentially committed murder. Jesus' brother James said, further, that he who allows his God-given natural desires to draw him away from the purposes of God to which he has committed himself, has sown the seeds of ambivalence, which can result in physical violence. He who allows unresolved guilt and conflict to remain within him is the father of war. Although this is true of everyone, we should notice that he said this to Christians.

In the next chapter we shall see the evidence that James had some reference to compulsion neurosis. Then we shall be ready to see the light which he saw at the end of the long dark cave.

Summary

Aggression in inter-personal relations can come from a number of sources. One of these is the unrestrained, natural reaction to frustration. This is not really the subject of James's fourth chapter. Another source is the series of three kinds of avoidance of a real inner problem. These are *scapegoating*, which is punishing others for one's own vague feeling of anxiety; *reaction formation*, which is acting in a manner opposite to the real inner problem in such a way as to conceal its character; and *projection*, which is seeing in others what is true of one's unconscious self. All of these can and do come from inner problems which are not consciously realized. Therefore they are a psychologist's filling-in between the lines of the first verse of the fourth chapter of James.

Aggression does not always succeed in attaching itself to an outside object, but sometimes turns in upon the person himself, so that he does himself damage — even though he is not thereby dealing with the real problem. The battle for our souls is indeed a fierce one, and James is right in saying that in both inter-personal and inter-group relationships, wars begin in the warring desires of the individual heart.

> *From whence come wars and fightings among you? come they not hence, even of your lusts that war in your members? Ye lust, and have not: ye kill, and desire to have, and cannot obtain: ye fight and war, yet ye have not, because ye ask not. Ye ask, and receive not, because ye ask amiss, that ye may consume it upon your lusts. Ye adulterers and adulteresses, know ye not that the friendship of the world is enmity with God? whosoever therefore will be a friend of the world is the enemy of God. Do ye think that the scripture saith in vain, The spirit that dwelleth in us lusteth to envy? But he giveth more grace. Wherefore he saith, God resisteth the proud, but giveth grace unto the humble. Submit yourselves therefore to God. Resist the devil, and he will flee from you.*
>
> James 4:1-7

6

PRESCRIPTION FOR HEALING

Before we can make any sort of prescription for the healing of mental illness, we must travel to the end of the dark road we have been on. We must see just how powerful are the forces which bind the double-minded person. Only when we know the worst about an illness will we be able to find the right cure. In order to do this we will discuss compulsion and obsession, two forms of neurotic behavior, and we will be following the route that James takes.

But first we need to take a brief but necessary side trip. Some people have suggested that what psychologists call mental illness is really demon possession. There certainly are some striking parallels between what is called neurosis and what is called demon possession. Let us notice some of them, limiting the discussion of certain aspects which seem useful to our understanding of neurotic obsession and compulsion.

Demon Possession and Neurosis

At the present stage of the development of psychology, we are not able to say in psychological language just what demon possession may be, nor how it relates to what we call mental illness. It is only natural that humanistic psychologists should brush it aside as an ancient superstition which has no objective reality. The truth is that no properly qualified person has ever really tried to find out if there is such a thing as a demon possession which can be understood or identified psychologically. Evangelical Christians believe that both the Old and New Testaments make valid observations in this respect, and that the biblical association of certain behavioral abnormalities with religious motivation is correct. It is not the object of this chapter to discuss demon possession except as it has some relevance to our subject of double-mindedness.

In his recent writings, O. Hobart Mowrer makes the point that there are some interesting parallels between what we call neurosis and what the Bible calls demon possession. One of these is that the cause of the neurosis is often a pull between two opposing, inner forces (as we have been saying). He says that these forces are always in a battle between good and evil (a statement which compares at least in part with psychoanalytic findings). Most psychologists tend to feel, however, that the struggle can equally well be between two good goals which are mutually exclusive. So even at the surface of the problem it would appear that some kinds of ambivalence may not be easy to relate to demon possession.

But whatever the case, the need to make a choice becomes a matter of such importance to the personality that the mere resolution of the problem becomes an ethical imperative. That is to say, even when the choice is between two good things which we want to possess (or follow or be), still the choice must be made, and to halt between the two becomes evil. To the Christian this evil takes on the force of sin — that is, a transgression against the will of God. Often enough the choice involves sufficient of good on one side and evil on the other that we can at least liken it to the struggle between God and the devil for our souls.

Another parallel between neurosis and demon possession

is that in both cases the person feels he is being driven by an uncontrollable force which works within him but is somehow not a part of himself. In psychological language this is called by the very suggestive terms, "compulsion" and "obsession." All neurotic behavior (of which we have given only a few generalized descriptions) has in it some elements of compulsion or of obsession. The phobia seems, to the neurotic, to force itself upon him. The bodily ailment seems to afflict him, not to come from himself. The memory seems just to have fled and he is powerless to do anything about it. He is quite at a loss to understand why he is two persons rather than one. James has chosen a very useful word when he says such a person is "*driven*" by the wind.

At this point, then, we leave the discussion of demon possession, perhaps with more questions than we had before, but probably with better questions. There are spots along the way where what we know will be of at least a little help.

The Nature of Compulsion and Obsession

Let us continue with the discussion of the psychological way of viewing the problem. It is characteristic of certain anxious people to be compulsive. They may speak explosively, find it necessary to explain excessively, have a need to pick their fingers or clothing, feel compelled to speak at every possible occasion, or perhaps have a great need to confess upon embarrassing subjects or occasions.

Sometimes such compulsion-motivated behavior may appear to be of an ethically commendable sort, but the trouble is that since the motivation is an unresolved and unconscious problem, this same motivation can at the next moment also drive the neurotic to behavior which is not ethically good. James is aware of such confused springs of behavior in some persons and says, "... *this should not be so. Does a fountain gush with fresh and brackish water from the same opening?"* (3:11, NEB).

In this manner some people are constantly driven to testify. There are people who normally say what is important to them, or what they think will be important to their hearers, and they do it only when they have something to be said — however often that may be. There are others who are driven to testify in a kind of ritualistic manner, as though there were a great, irrational and uncontrollable inner need to do it. Usually these people speak with a strong sense of duty or "oughtness" and very little genuine pleasure (except that a semblance of pleasure may be drummed up for the sake of the listeners). At times they even feel downright foolish or hypocritical, but the need to go through the motions is much too strong to resist. They feel bad until they do it, and may not feel much better when they have done it, yet they must go through the performance. They appear to be driven rather than led, and their theory states that an impulse to do so good a thing as to testify (even when there is nothing worth testifying about) could come only from the leading of the Holy Spirit. This puts them into considerable difficulty. When they do not testify they feel they are resisting the Holy Spirit. When they do testify, they feel that their obedience is not sufficiently quick to His prodding and therefore they have no joy, only constant condemnation, even though they have done what they were compelled to do. Once again there are congregations, and even denominations which, by their teachings, accumulate neurotics with this kind of behavior.

I remember a prominent Christian woman in one such congregation who came for help with her problems. Among other things she spoke of her great need to testify, the great emotion with which she testified, the great doubts she had about her honesty in the testimony, and the utter bewilderment and powerlessness which she experienced in the whole situation. This particular person not only had compulsive characteristics, but had experienced mild psychotic behavior at times.

The result of too much of this kind of compulsive religious behavior can give a weird feeling of a foreign power around such a church, and after a while this does not feel like the power of the God whom the Bible reveals, but very much akin to the power that moves in a mental hospital ward.

The empty, compulsive, repetitive performance of what should be a spontaneous, creative, and consciously directed activity, is not really what Christianity seeks. God, according to the Scriptures, prefers always to work in cooperation with the consciously self-directing mind which is in full control of its faculties, and which has chosen Him as the Way. This leaves plenty of room for the guidance of the Holy Spirit. It leaves room for a Christian to do better than he knows, because God gives him wisdom beyond his knowledge. But it leaves very little room for the human "zombie" type of automatic performance, which by some uninformed people is regarded as a manifestation of the presence of the Holy Spirit. It is impossible to support from the Bible the idea that when the Holy Spirit guides a person he is less intellectually keen, perceptive and oriented to reality than when he is not divinely guided. God heightens men's powers, He does not deaden them. Paul, the bondslave of Jesus Christ, was if anything a more intellectual person than Saul the slave of sin.

An obsession is a persistent and irrational idea, usually unpleasant (though not always), that comes into consciousness inappropriately and cannot be banished by an effort of the will. Thus a person is not in control of his thoughts, but possessed by them. The thoughts persist in coming for no under-standable reason. They intrude as unpleasant visitors and will not go away. They just stay there, strange and unwelcome guests who have forced themselves into our awareness, and persist in dominating consciousness against anything we may try to do to dislodge them.

Not every persistent thought is a neurotic obsession. The question, "Did I really turn off the water in the sink?" may be based on actual previous negligence. The haunting thought of coming examinations may relate quite properly to a very real event that presents some very real threats. These persistent thoughts may, therefore, have some good reason, which can be understood, which is related to reality, and which will diminish when the appropriate action or time comes. The true obsession is a thought like, "The kiss of death is sweet," or "Sex is Satan," or perhaps the nagging and nonunderstandable phrase, "Go forth and proclaim filth upon the highways."

God is not a God of unreasonableness, nor of confusion. The Scriptures teach us that He is more willing to make Him-self clearly understood than we are to understand. It is not characteristic of God to do things darkly and in corners. Whether it be by the clear word of the prophets, or by the forceful reasonableness of the written Bible, or by the clearly comprehensible character of Jesus, God seeks always to in-clude an appeal to the best of man's rational powers in every revelation of Himself. Satan loves darkness, obscurity and confusion, but not God. Even concerning the mysteries of spiritual revelation He says, "Come now, and let us reason together" (Isaiah 1:18). Therefore, one may speculate as to what relationship neurotic obsession has to demonic posses-sion. It is rather sure that the neurotic feels himself possessed by something outside himself, and this something behaves in a way that makes us doubt that it is God.

The neurotic compulsions we have considered are much like the obsessions. Compulsions are "bizarre and incomprehensible actions which have no observable value and which the individual himself does not understand, but which press for expression in a most uncomfortable and compelling way. . . . Compulsions are usually symbolic — that is, the patient resorts to the compulsive reaction as an indirect way of resolving some anxiety or repressed desire. Most commonly, compulsions take the form of 'rituals,' or extremely detailed preoccupation with minor, everyday tasks. For example, guilt feelings arising from stealing or masturbation may lead to frequent, compulsive hand-washing in a symbolic attempt to 'wash away' the guilt."[1]

Hand-washing! That strikes a familiar note. There it is in the verse that follows James's discussion about scapegoating as a result of unresolved inner conflicts. "*Cleanse your hands, ye sinners; and purify your hearts ye double minded*" (4:8). Or as the New English Bible renders it ". . . *see that your motives are pure.*"

How well this fits a discussion of compulsive neurosis. Did James have neurotic hand-washing compulsion in mind? Whatever he had in mind, it fits well into our continuing parallel discussions of neurosis and biblical double-mindedness.

At first glance the Bible student will recognize that this is a paraphrase of that Old Testament description of personality integration: "Who shall ascend into the hill of the Lord? or who shall stand in his holy place? He that hath clean hands, and a pure heart; who hath not lifted up his soul unto vanity, nor sworn deceitfully" (Psalm 24:3,4).

---

[1]Floyd L. Ruch, *Psychology and Life. Fourth Edition.* Chicago: Scott, Foresman, and Company, 1953, p. 167. This definition is clearer than the one in the fifth edition.

It was when I saw the relationship of James's statement to the following comment by Freud, that there resulted the chain of thoughts out of which this book was born. Freud says, "The form in which taboo manifests itself has the greatest similarity to the touching phobia of neurotics, the *delire de toucher*."[2] Then there comes to mind our previous illustration of the neurotic cat that could not bring itself to touch the pole. And then one sees that this statement by James is more than a casual reference to a familiar Old Testament psalm. It has real meaning in his discussion of double-mindedness.

Notice, now, this longer quotation from the same article by Freud,

> . . . when we have learnt that the obsessive rules of certain neurotics are nothing but measures of self-assurance and self-punishment erected against the reinforced impulse to commit murder, we can return with fresh appreciation to our previous hypothesis that every prohibition must conceal a desire. We can then assume that this desire to murder actually exists and that the taboo as well as the moral prohibition are psychologically by no means superfluous but are on the contrary, explained through our ambivalent attitude towards the impulse to slay.[3]

I hold that it is no coincidence that both Freud and James bring murder, hand-washing, and ambivalence together in a single paragraph. They are clearly related, and both writers recognized it.

It is very likely that James witnessed at least one memorable exhibition of hand-washing which had symbolic meaning. We know that James and his brothers went up to the Passover feasts in Jerusalem (John 7:1-10), and it is very probable they were also in Jerusalem for the Passover during which Christ was arrested, tried and crucified. So he may have watched Pilate perform his hand-washing ceremony. Whether this

---

[2]Freud, *op. cit.*, p. 863.
[3]*Ibid.*, p. 861.

hand-washing is done publicly as a recognized common ritual such as this, or whether it is done deliriously at night like Lady Macbeth does it in Shakespeare's play or whether it is repeated in the family bathroom by a guilty adolescent, it still has the same essential meaning. It expresses the desire to rid one's self symbolically of guilt, and we see it often in the compulsive neurotic.

Hand-washing has its legitimate, practical purposes. A dentist told me that one day he counted that he washed his hands fifty-three times at his office — to prevent infection as he went from one person's mouth to another. This is obviously unrelated to compulsive hand-washing. The compulsive person may wash his hands dozens of times a day but never brush his teeth. It is said that a former dean of women in a Christian college would not touch so much as the doorknobs without gloves on her hands and that a professor in another Christian college would never handle even the students' assigned papers with his "naked" hands. He always wore gloves wherever he went, and when he took them off, eye-witnesses say he had a method of going through papers with something like a combination of the elbow and the back of his hand. Though these people may never have committed an act anywhere as evil as their action suggests, they would appear to have exhibited compulsive preoccupation with cleanliness such as is typically symbolic of a deeper inner problem.

James uses his quotation from Psalm 24 in a psychologically perceptive manner which suggests the depth of his insight. Notice the way he combines the elements. He says, "*Cleanse your hands, you sinners,*" and then adds the typical Hebrew parallelism in which the same, or a similar thought, is repeated: "*Purify your hearts, you double minded.*" He found it easy to think together of hand-washing and heart-washing. It is as though he were saying to the compulsive hand-washer, "You are washing your hands, not because they are physically dirty, but because of a vague need to deal with your sinfulness." Sinfulness and soiled hands are a common Old Testament simile. And to the double-minded he is saying, "You are torn by conflict because your heart is not clean, your motives are not pure" — that is, they are mixed. To sum it up, James is saying that double-mindedness and the accompanying neurotic behavior come to an end when the person is inwardly clean, whole, correctly directed or integrated — and, of course, that is the theme of the whole epistle, into which this part fits so well.

So What Can We Do About It?

But wait. I can hear the minds clicking at this point and saying, "Aha, I knew it! He took us the long way around Robin Hood's barn, but he finally came out the same door as all the others. So, we're supposed to be good children and do as the preacher says!"

Not quite. Don't forget that I have pointed out all along that often we cannot be good children and do as the preacher says. I have said that the extent to which one is neurotic is likely to be also the extent to which one's problem has been repressed into the area of the unconscious where one cannot get at it or even recognize it.

Jesus said, "Blessed are the pure in heart: for they shall see God" (Matthew 5:8). James has made a similar statement here, *"Draw nigh to God and he will draw nigh to you . . . purify your hearts, ye double minded"* (4:8). But he has previously pointed out that the person with mixed motives (an impure heart) will not see God. Having promised that God will give wisdom generously (1:5), James continues by saying that the one who asks with doubt or wavering is a double-minded person who will receive nothing from the Lord (1:6) — evidently not even the wisdom he needs. Or, as a psychiatrist said recently about the treatment of neurosis, "It takes a great deal of emotional maturity to be able to see one's emotional immaturity well enough to be willing to do something about it."

Now you may well say, "What an impossibility! We will have to clean out things which we can't even see to clean out." Exactly. That is just what psychology says, and I am convinced that James says it too. At this point we have arrived at the nadir of the descent in our Pilgrim's Regress. We are at the bottom. It is exactly that impossible, hopeless and futile. The only way out from here that I know, either as a Christian or as a psychologist, is for the neurotic to pass through this degrading eye of the needle. He must be willing to admit that the problem is entirely beyond his control, and that it is not just a little problem but a very large one. Alcoholics Anonymous recognizes this necessity and refuses to take a member who thinks he can help himself. Alcoholism, incidentally, for whatever else it is, is now recognized as a neurotic way to deal with a hidden inner problem. Let me suggest that we need to join a sort of Sinners Anonymous, and it should have a membership comprising the entire church of Christ.

It is not for nothing that the psalmist says, "Search me, O God, and know my heart: try me, and know my thoughts: And see if there be any wicked way in me." (Psalm 139:23, 24). The fact is that we don't do too good a job of searching ourselves. Our eyes are too easily closed to the real problems by the problems themselves. That is why the psalmist does not search his own heart in this instance, but calls upon outside help.

If it seems unnecessarily repetitious to emphasize here what the church has always preached, let it be said that whereas there have always been some preachers of righteousness who have included this in their message; and whereas their audiences have commonly nodded in agreement, it has not always been well understood or accepted in practice.

We have somehow assumed that even though we speak of non-Christians as "helpless sinners," "lost in darkness," "astray from the fold of God," and quote the verse which tells us that the preaching of the cross is foolishness to the lost (who cannot understand it), yet we have behaved as though such lost people should be able to help themselves. This manifests itself in various statements, which, when brought together, say, "You are helpless. . . . Stop it"; "You are a sinner. . . . Stop it"; "You are hopelessly enmeshed in sin which has overpowered you, and blinded your eyes, and over which you have no control. . . . Stop it."

In other words, *we* are blind to our attitudes toward others. And we are blind to our blindness! We are generally unaware that we, too, are unable to see very deeply into our own motives.

Since this last is true, let us not try to see ourselves. Rather let us talk about how we see others — that is much easier. If each of us sees the other correctly, then in the end all will be helped.

Unfortunately, when the sinner has opened the least bit of his problem to us in confidence, we have actually been shocked. But according to our own doctrines, what else did we expect to find? When the sinner has come to us and opened his heart, we have been shocked at his sin, and have reprimanded him. What help is that? What does it assume? To the person who was ridden with shame, who came to us for help, we have said, "You should be ashamed of yourself!" And, unfortunately, even ministers have been known to try to make themselves

feel more righteous at the expense of being shocked at someone else's sin.

This matter of being so shocked at sin that we cannot be
of help to the sinner is a real problem with many Christians.
Behind this shock there is frequently a reaction formation
such as was discussed in chapter 5. For example, I remember
a rather typical case of a married woman, very prim, erect
and neat, who came for help with a child that was having
difficulty. (This is a rather common way of projecting our
problems onto someone else — the child has troubles.) Her
sugary sweet reasonableness and her lengthy descriptions of
how carefully she had tried to raise this child became rather
tiring after a while. I tried to shut her off because I already
knew much more than I could use, but she had a great need
to make her own purity quite clear. In the course of the conversation she managed to speak at length about the shocking
immorality of certain other people, until I began to squirm
with her at the sea of filth with which she perceived herself
as being surrounded. I discovered later that I had not been the
first professional person to suggest to her that she needed psychotherapy for her own inner problems. As far as I know,
she never went for help, but kept on looking for assistance
for her child — who would likely have been quite normal
if his mother would have behaved more rationally. Unfortunately, mother had a need to be terribly shocked and to
stay in a position where she could be shocked. (Unfortunately,
many are counselors — both in and out of the church — from
this very motivation.)

Not only have we reacted with shock to the confessions
of the sinner, but we have also acted as though those inside
the church should be lily-white angels. As a result, how few

of us church members have the courage to admit to anyone that we too have inner problems and conflicts and guilt.

Just to illustrate how vicious this has become among us who hold ourselves to be so holy, let me ask this question: "Where can a minister in your denomination go in order to confess his sin?" Isn't it true that there is usually no person whom he would dare to trust with such information? It's a wonder more ministers aren't mentally ill.

And it is no wonder that many of the deepest and most real problems in churches and individuals have not been exposed. No wonder that we have so many formalistic "conversions" which are not a real rooting out of the basic problems and an integration of life. Too many people have learned that they dare not trust the Christian to have genuine sympathy and to give unselfish help, so they go through whatever it is that the church expects them to do. Having gone through this performance (which may have much the same significance as the symbolic hand-washing) they go on helplessly with their neuroses.

It is not for nothing that I seem to get an upswing in counseling clients after revival meetings, usually persons who obediently "went forward." This is no depreciation of revival meetings, but of the way they are sometimes conducted. The symptoms with which they come may be in a form which are disguised as something far from religion; or they may be symptoms of religious problems which are disguises for things which are even harder for the client to face, and which in the end are not unrelated to problems of good and evil.

Another of the ways in which the church has sometimes failed to live up to its own preaching that the soul is helpless alone, is the way in which it has shrugged off certain problems as being unimportant. One hears such vicious and unsympathetic remarks as, "It's all in your head." But since the brain is what it is, *every* spiritual problem must to a real degree be in the head.

If a man has crippled hands we do not expect him to pass out the song books, saying, "It's only in your hands." No more can we expect a person whose brain is under the emotional strain and malfunction of a neurosis to operate as an effective Christian, for, as we have seen earlier, the personality is a unity in which every part is affected by that which affects any part of it. It is artificial to try to separate mental or emotional problems too completely from spiritual problems, even though there are some specialized aspects of each which are different from the other.

There is a great place for evangelism in our time, but, to repeat an earlier emphasis, it seems that the text for our neurotic age is that gently pleading one in which Jesus stands at the door and knocks, seeking fellowship and promising "To him who is victorious I will grant a place on my throne, as I myself was victorious and sat down with my Father on his throne" (Revelation 3:21, NEB). Without minimizing the sin, Jesus invites the sinner. James says, "*Brothers, you must never disparage one another*" (4:11, NEB).

The preacher of righteousness must still hold forth truth and decry evil, even as James does so forcibly. Yet there is a new evangelism in our time, which is not conducted from the pulpit but which has a powerful appeal to sinners. If you could sit with any clinical psychologist for an afternoon you might see people who never think of going to a revival meeting. All the psychologist needs to do is to sit there, perhaps mercifully not even looking into the face of the patient (following the custom of psychoanalysts), and these people pour out their flood of evil and the despair at their own helplessness, while he listens with sympathy. They are open at the deepest levels of the personality, levels which a great majority of ministers never have an opportunity to discover. But the listener must be to them what the word minister means — a servant. He cannot be a boss, or a director, or a judge. He must take his cues from the Christ who said he was sent into the world, not to condemn the world, but that the world through Him might be saved (John 3:17).

In all that I have been saying there is little by way of new ideas. There is, however, something very new by way of understanding why these long-standing Christian teachings are so basically correct — and understanding the sort of attitudes in which Christians should exercise the beliefs they have verbalized so long. Perhaps they sound new as they come from the psychoanalyst, only because so much of Christianity has lost what it once had. James makes it look as though the struggle to get these attitudes has always been present with the church. He says, *"Brothers, you must never disparage one another,"* and we notice that he says this after he has laid open the sources of scapegoating and compulsive behavior.

It is in recognizing the reasons for and the validity of this statement that we find ourselves on our way to catch the first gleam of hope for the double-minded person. It is possible to cleanse the soul, to cure double-mindedness, to wash the hands from the inside so that they remain clean.

Here, as elsewhere in the Bible, we are faced with the paradox of the helplessness of the individual together with his personal responsibility. To remain entirely practical, we must say that this same paradox faces any person who is neurotic, whether his problem is spiritual or not. The neurotic is unable to help himself, and therefore he needs the help of others. In the same way, the physically ill person cannot help himself and needs the help of others. In both cases, there remains an element of individual responsibility without which healing cannot occur. A person must be willing to admit that he needs help, he must seek out a qualified person to help him, and he must cooperate with that person. James says in this part of his epistle, *"Submit yourselves therefore to God"* (4:7), and *"Humble yourselves in the sight of the Lord, and he shall lift you up"* (4:10).

James will show us that he does not mean God will do it as an automatic result of any kind of humbling. He has further methodology to bring forth. God does the healing, but He does it with the help of certain people, and by certain approved methods. The evangelical is once again prone to oversimplification, and may say, as I heard someone say to a neurotic, "Let's pray. We have a God who is sufficient for every need." As a general summary this is correct, but it does the neurotic no more specific good than to say to a person, "What you need is medicine for your ailment." He needs a specific kind of medicine, applied in a very correct way, and probably by a highly trained specialist. The same God who has specific rules which must be followed to heal the body has specific rules by which the healing of the mind can come. It is our business to learn them. If this study of James accomplishes nothing else, it should at least show that psychological techniques are compatible with the Bible, and indeed suggested by the Bible. It is impossible to impart in these few chapters the amount of information and method which it takes a clinical psychologist eight years of hard study to master, but one can at least give a few rules by which the psychological layman can administer "first aid." If the ailment is not too severe, "first aid" may be sufficient. If it is severe, perhaps his knowledge will help him to recognize the severity and cause him to be the one who will urge and help the sufferer to get assistance from more technically trained persons.

In moving toward James's suggestions for healing, notice the words which follow in the fourth chapter, and which we have already mentioned. It is immediately after he has asked his readers to humble themselves before God that he says we must never disparage each other. This is a fine psychological sequence. The passage is directed straight at the pastor's wife who, knowing that I am a psychologist, said to me in a voice that left no doubt about how juicy such information would be to her, "You must hear a lot of *very* interesting things about people."

At the risk of redundancy let us say that James is quite logical in implying that if the sufferer is to humble himself before God, admit his weakness and look for help, it will also require brethren who, like God, have the graciousness not to look down their noses, or pry, or scold. This is a simple, unspectacular and unmysterious prescription for the healing ministry of the church. The loving and wise among us have already known and practiced this. They have not needed the validation of psychology. But now that we have it, we have a better understanding of why some of the right methods have worked. Perhaps we will now be in position to do consciously and in greater numbers what some people have done all along. The next chapter will explore some ways in which this principle of acceptance works and how it can be applied to some specific problems which are the concern of James.

Acceptance is such a simple truth, but I rather doubt that people ever learn it from books. Love is learned from people who love. In recognition of this, God who had commanded

His people, "Thou shalt love," for a whole millenium, finally sent forth His Son in order that men might learn about love in person.

Summary

Whatever demon possession may be, neurosis has similarities at several points. The person feels driven, and by a force which is at the same time within him yet not of him. Obsessions, which dominate people's thoughts against their will, and compulsions which cause them to do irrational things, both tend to express some inner problem in a symbolic manner. This is notably true of the hand-washing compulsion which may be a symbolic cleansing for inner feelings of hostility, sexual guilt, or other kinds of "uncleanness." Psychological theory and practice point out that where an underlying ambivalence is the source of compulsive behavior, such as hand-washing, the relief of the symptom comes from a resolution of the ambivalence. James similarly says that the solution to hand-washing is the achievement of unmixed — pure — motivation. James further points out that the sufferer should be treated with acceptance, regardless of how one may feel about his behavior. Once again, he is in agreement with accepted psychological methodology.

> *Draw nigh to God, and he will draw nigh to you. Cleanse your hands, ye sinners; and purify your hearts, ye double minded. . . . Humble yourselves in the sight of the Lord, and he shall lift you up. Speak not evil one of another, brethren. . . .*   James 4:8, 10, 11

7

THE HEALING OF THE WHOLE PERSON

The Bible has never taught the kind of dichotomy between physical and mental illness which has been permitted to invade our churches and our culture as a whole. In the effort to restore proper concepts of the relationship between them, psychology, psychiatry, physiology, and other disciplines have made some important discoveries and pronouncements. The clergy must help in the process and resume their share in the healing ministry which the church has so largely abandoned. Fortunately, there is already a growing literature on this subject by religious leaders as well as by others, so this book can confine itself to those insights which fit closely into the subject at hand.

In the previous chapter there was laid a foundation upon which to base the discussion of healing. In this, and the following chapter, healing and health are carried as far as they seem to be treated in the epistle of James. Once again, we proceed by means of a parallel discussion of neurosis from the psychological standpoint and double-mindedness as discussed by James.

It is of some value to notice that as we have discussed the ambivalent sources of neurotic behavior, then the development and manifestation of the symptoms themselves, so we have also moved from the first part of the epistle through the several chapters, with very little doubling back except to re-emphasize early passages in their relationship to later ones. Herein lies another parallel of the book of James with psychology. It presents its materials (embedded as they are in the larger text of the epistle) in a sequence which is very much like that in which one would develop an orderly classroom, or textbook discussion of the causes, symptoms and cure of neurosis.

We must constantly keep in mind that James did not propose to write a textbook on neurosis, and that double-mindedness is only the negative side of one of the major themes of the book. That it should fall so easily into a recognizable pattern shows only that his thinking allows for these insights, and not that he tries to make an exhaustive study of them. If at places I have picked out the secondary rather than the primary meaning of a sentence, I propose that such a secondary meaning is nevertheless intended. At places I tend to disagree with what others have regarded as secondary meanings of the text, and feel that we have overlooked primary meanings.

Some Roots of Neurotic Behavior

It is well that we have spent so much time in getting an understanding of the roots and behavior of neurotic problems. Because we know them, we may be able to avoid many pitfalls in the attempt to offer salvation to the double-minded.

Now let us review a number of the important principles that have been discussed earlier, in order to see how they may be applied in our discussion of healing. We have said that:

1. When a person is caught between competing ways of life in such a way that he cannot resolve the conflict, the result is a great deal of emotional stress.

2. If the stress is great and no solution is apparent, the whole

problem may be driven into the unconscious.

3. Even though the problem is not conscious, it is still present.

4. A problem in one part of a person affects the total personality, including those areas which we speak of as physical, mental, emotional, spiritual, social, or whatever ways we have of classifying aspects of a person.

5. The fact that the problem has been repressed into the unconscious, and therefore cannot be dealt with at the conscious level, often results in expressions which the person himself does not understand, and which we call the symptoms of neurotic behavior. These are such things as a general nameless anxiety, loss of memory, the irrational fears called phobias, the irrational drives called obsessions and compulsions, and finally a number of reactions which give a false appearance of physical disorder, such as fatigue, strong concerns about general illness, and also the experience of specific ailments when the supposed diseased parts of the body show no physical damage or malfunction.

6. We specially noted that among the neurotic ways in which the personality may defend the conscious mind against becoming aware of the internal (unconscious) conflicts are the defenses of scapegoating, and symbolic hand-washing.

7. All these neurotic defenses arise from divided motives (impure in the sense that they are mixed). For the Christian, these divided motives are indeed impure and sinful, for the primary commandment of both the Old and the New Testaments is, "The Lord our God is one Lord: and thou shalt love the Lord thy God with all thy heart, and with all thy soul, and with all . . . thy strength. . ." (Mark 12:29, 30).

For these principles we found parallel statements in the epistle.

It is important to recognize once more the fact that if there are causes of neurosis which do not involve conflicts of good and evil, and some measure of personal choice, James does not seem to deal with them, though he does not exclude them either.

It may be, as the psychoanalysts say, that there are causes of mental illness which are not the fault of the individual, but of his early childhood environment. If so, the Bible is quite agreed that the spiritual ills of man come both from his fore-bears and from himself, for "in Adam all die" (I Corinthians 15:22) and "as by one man sin entered into the world, and death by sin; and so death passed upon all men, for that all have sinned" (Romans 5:12). It is probably both good theology and good psychology to paraphrase these verses as saying, "It was the spiritual (or mental) illness of one man that caused all men to become ill in turn, as each one, under the influence of his parents, personally repeated such acts as caused him to be sick."

Let me admit that this is a debatable theological position, and get away from it in order to return to the more certain ground of the text of the epistle. We will have to return to this question once more, however. Meanwhile, the psychologist at least (and doubtless some theologians) will be delighted to observe that James treats the sinner as though he were indeed not able to help himself. Later in this discussion we will find that the double-minded person does not effect his own cure, but only calls for help. Leaving questions of the prevenient work of the Holy Spirit for some other discussion, we notice that James is quite ready to accept the same degree of individual responsibility as is the psychotherapist — namely, the patient must ask for treatment and must cooperate while it is being given. But now we are ahead of ourselves.

Other disorders of a more serious kind do exist, but James does not seem to talk about the psychoses, so we must confine ourselves to those which are stated or implied by the biblical text.

We need to remember now that in the mind-body relationship the entire personality is affected by the illness of the human spirit. Some of these interrelationships have been noted, but others must be dealt with.

The Interrelationship of Mind and Body

Throughout the Bible there is indicated a clear relationship between the illness of the spirit and the illness of the body. Psychology and medicine have come to an increasingly detailed study of these relationships.

Going back to what was said before, we can name at least three broad causes of physical ailments. There are those purely physical causes which I am unqualified to discuss and to which physicians appropriately apply physical remedies. Even concerning these the physician recognizes that a good frame of mind is important to recovery, even though the mental state may not have been involved in the cause.

The second general class is that which was discussed before; the vague feelings of illness when there really is no illness. These are called neurasthenic symptoms and hypochondriacal symptoms, and may also include the symptoms of specific illnesses for which there is no physical cause, which are called conversion hysteria symptoms. You will recall the case of supposed appendicitis which recurred even when there wasn't an appendix. In the same manner almost every ailment which is classified has at some time or other been experienced by someone, without any observable physical cause, and many have been cured without physical means.

To the person who feels that he is paralyzed in his right arm, this causes him to lose the function of that arm. If the cause is "all in his head" that doesn't make any difference. If he has lost the use of his eyes, or ears, or has become unable to speak, these are indeed disabilities which are, for him, just as real as if they had a physical cause. When we call these "conversion reactions," we mean that the person is transforming or converting a disturbance of the emotions or mind into a physical problem. Often a physical problem is easier to bear than the spiritual problem which one is trying to escape. That is already a familiar concept to the reader of the earlier chapters.

Speaking now about healing, it is easy to see that if such a person achieves that wholehearted, confident, dedicated directedness which leaves him no ambivalence and which we call faith, then his spiritual problem has been healed. It is also easy to see how this would then make the physical symptoms unnecessary. Such a person would, and does, experience a physical healing just as much as he experienced a physical illness. This is a real faith healing. Having healed the faith, the other healing follows as a matter of course. Let no one despise such faith healing, for it occurs often, both in the psychological clinic, in the church, and in the private hour of prayer. It is a real healing to someone who has suffered, regardless of what others may think of it.

Notice a pitfall, however. If the person went about to have his physical symptom healed, he could probably achieve this without knowing what caused it or how he got healed. Since he consciously experiences only a physical ailment which is not physically caused, all he needs in order to be "healed" is to have a change in the symptoms. Unfortunately, there are many for whom this happens. They say they are healed, and so they are in a way, but all that has been healed is the problem at the surface — the physical complaint. God and the unconscious demand a deeper healing than that. Usually these same people are back for healing again very soon. The real problem is still there. It is no less painful than before, and the person has had no help to remove it, so it demands a new expression in some other form of hysterical illness.

Such people are excellent subjects for faith healing meetings, because the supposed faith healer, if he heals the symptoms without healing the spirit, can heal these people repeatedly and get greater and greater glory in the process. Such people in fact, would, rather be healed of the symptoms than of the deeper cause. If these people could unload their burden to some sympathetic brother or sister, they might get at the real problem, and there might occur, without any meetings at all, the true faith healing — the healing of the faith which dries up the roots from which the symptoms have grown.

This is one of the reasons that James insists upon sympathetic listening as being of utmost importance. It still leaves us with many questions of method unanswered, but we must be satisfied that we have also got some meaningful insights into both James and mental healing.

A third class of illnesses is the sort in which there is a real physical ailment, which, however, is either caused entirely by a problem of the mind, or which has been aggravated by such a mental problem. Once again, the healer can be sidetracked into an endless curing of symptoms without ever getting at the real illness. We are all aware of the statements which are made about the very high proportion of stomach ulcers which come from emotional disturbance as the original cause. (Please remember that some stomach ulcers are the result of physical causes, and do not make the mistake of deciding hastily what has caused your ulcers, or those of someone you know. By all means go to a physician who you know will give full recognition to both possible causes, and who will see to it that you are referred to the proper kind of help in either case.)

With regard to this third kind of psychosomatic illness, Hans Selye has apparently discovered a link between the mind and the body. You will find his book, *The Stress of Life,* fascinating reading, even though you may not be too well oriented in chemistry or physiology. He calls this link the General Adaptation Syndrome. Although it cannot be discussed in full here, we can get an outline.

He says that when a person, or an animal, is under any kind of stress, the endocrine glands react in such a way that there is a general "alarm reaction." We have already alluded, in a general way, to the fact that in anger or fear the adrenal cortex secretes more adrenalin into the blood stream than usual, to make us act more quickly, more strongly, with greater endurance and less pain than when we are not thus motivated. Other glands become involved as well. If the cause of stress is not removed, says Selye, the alarm reaction continues for about twenty-four hours. By that time the endocrine gland system goes through some further adjustive reactions and goes into what he calls the "stage of resistance." In this stage, which may continue almost indefinitely, the body does not return to normal, but a constant stream of hormones mobilizes the total resources of the body to react against the cause of the stress, in order to protect the body. During this time the person may appear, outwardly, to be normal, in spite of the inner battle.

Selye says that the reaction is the same if a person is continually taking a sub-lethal dose of poison (almost any kind of poison), suffering from too much cold or heat, losing too much sleep over a long period of time, working too hard for a long period of time, worrying, angry, or afraid. In each case, the same process goes on in the body, involving the same glands. The list of causes is far from complete, but we have included those which concern this discussion. In each case something may finally break down under the strain of the chemical imbalance in the blood stream. What breaks down seems to be determined by what part of the body of this individual is the weakest, and not by the kind of strain which is causing the reaction. So, we see that the entire body — every organ and the whole blood stream — is affected by that unresolved conflict which our neurotic person has tucked away in what he thought was the basement of his mind.

If the stress continues long enough and strong enough, the whole body finally exhausts its resources, the original alarm reaction returns, and usually death follows in a matter of hours or days. Thus, within the framework of this discussion as well as in other ways, "... *sin, when it is finished, bringeth forth death*" (1:15).

Selye says he has successfully killed experimental animals from each of the causes named above, and many more. He insists that the results are regularly the same. When an autopsy is performed it is always possible to identify a physical pathology which caused death; but, of course, the experimenter knows that behind the inflamed liver, the heart attack, the diseased colon or whatever it may be is another more basic cause.

It makes one wonder what lies behind some of the statements that are found on people's death certificates. Certainly he died of whatever the physician has named — but *why* did he die? How many cases of slow suicide are concealed behind physical symptoms?

James certainly was not aware of the technicalities of the General Adaptation Syndrome, and doubtless knew little or nothing of the adrenal cortex, but he hit the truth squarely when he traced temptation's effects through to death. Perhaps this little excursion into physiology will help us to keep the mind and body together both in sickness and in healing. Perhaps it can also point out a new way to life. Once again the healing of faith becomes a little more clear. And perhaps, even more than before, we can see that when James speaks of healing, we are in some ways justified in thinking of the healing of the mind, the spirit, and the body all at the same time, without too much attempt at distinction.

The Miracle of Healing

With this as a background, we can move with a new freedom and confidence to the words of James in his closing chapter:

> *Is anyone in good heart? He should sing praises. Is one of you ill? He should send for the elders of the congregation to pray over him and anoint him with oil in the name of the Lord. The prayer offered in faith will save the sick man, the Lord will raise him from his bed, and any sins he may have committed will be forgiven. Therefore confess your sins to one another, and pray for one another, and then you will be healed. A good man's prayer is powerful and effective* (5:13-16, NEB).

These are very nearly the closing words of the epistle.

Anyone who believes in God must believe in the possibility of miracles, or he has no God. But how unfortunate is the person who can see miracles only in what he does not understand! Such a person must protect his faith by ignorance. As for me, the more I understand, the more I marvel. For me, no explanation "explains away" anything. God's truth and God's methods are much more amazing to me than mysteries. One day "we shall be like him, for we shall see him as he is." I am sure that such a complete knowledge of Him as this implies will make Him more wonderful, rather than less. And if God in some small way puts some of the controls over some small part of

His wonderful creation in our hands, we do not honor Him by refusing to use those controls to glorify Him and to help our fellow men. When we have done all that we can do, there is still plenty of need and room for miracles of the mysterious kind. Let us not try to make mysteries out of things God wants us to understand. We tremble here at the brink of discovery, and we would not want to turn back to ignorance.

James puts all kinds of healing into the same package, just as we do in a thoroughly staffed clinic, where the physician, the social worker, the psychologist, and the minister all work together to help the patient. In James's day there were no physicians such as we know now, and so he asked his people to call on whom they had — the faithful brethren of the congregation. He knew that much healing could be done through them. Just as he indicated an awareness of the general outline of the causes and symptoms of neurosis, so he indicates an awareness of some principles of psychotherapy. In each case there is a great deal to be filled into the outline, for which we call upon psychology, but the outline is good, and by following it many have been helped before there was a formal psy-. chology.

Some Principles of Psychotherapy

From the practice of mental healing we need to gather several cardinal principles or concepts. One of these is the concept of catharsis. This means, in extremely nontechnical language, getting the rotten potatoes out of the cellar of one's mind. It is the process by which the sufferer speaks out whatever he finds in his mind. If he accomplishes an uncovering of the real problem, at least two things occur. One is that he is able to see the problem more clearly. The fact that he then knows what is really wrong makes it no longer necessary to continue the futile activities which have been the symptoms of his neurosis. Often, although not always, neurotic symptoms begin to drop away automatically. The other thing that happens is that he can now deal with the matter directly and consciously. He can try to understand how he got into this difficulty, what it really means to him, and under what circumstances he is likely to meet it again. He needs help for this, but he can at least start to understand how he really acts, and why. Knowing the cause can do for the sufferer what one student expressed: "I've always known this about people, but now all at once it's *me*." Until then his problem had been too hard to face. Now it was possible for him to get a more realistic grip on it.

A second concept of psychotherapy is that the hearer must accept the speaker. It is not too hard for us to see why this must be true. We have thought about it before. The rottenness of the soul does not want to expose itself any more than we would want to bring rotten potatoes out of the cellar and dump them in front of visiting friends. Don't ask why one wouldn't want to dump rotten potatoes before friends. (Have you ever smelled rotten potatoes?) Doubtless the question can be answered in words, but unless you can *feel* the answer to such a question you will need to develop a great deal before people will trust you with their deepest problems. For people who turn up their noses even at the smell of cooking cabbage, one will not bring out the worst inner rottenness. But that rottenness needs a catharsis and a catharsis demands truly accepting listeners.

Acceptance means at least two specific things. One is that we must never depreciate the size of the problem nor the blackness of the sin. Sins are as bad as they are, and no one is helped by pretending otherwise. In fact, unless you realize the blackness of his sin, the sufferer cannot trust you with it, because he is convinced you just don't understand. This was one of the weaknesses of the old liberal theology which minimized man's sinfulness and concentrated on the "spark of divinity" within him. This philosophy won't work in the clinic, and it didn't work in the pulpit.

On the other hand, acceptance means friendship with the sinner. Friendship can probably be described in no better way than in what someone has proposed as the definition of a friend — "A person who knows all about you and likes you anyway." In this mood the accepting listener says by his attitude, "Yes, you suffer much. Yes, the evil is great. Yes, you have felt deeply injured. Yes, you are overcome by this wickedness. But that does not change my attitude toward you at all." He may indeed say so in words. But however he communicates it, his attitude is clear and stated so consistently that the sufferer can believe it.

It is not practical to go much farther into therapeutic method here, since this is not a dissertation on psychotherapy. There is a book, however, which should be in every minister's library, and which should probably be read more than once in order to absorb its spirit. This is *Counseling and Psychotherapy*, by Carl Rogers. It is not his most recent book, but for this purpose is his best. I am also aware that psychoanalysts will cry out in horror at this point and say I have left their fold, but that does not matter either. It is not necessary to agree with everything Rogers says, nor with his whole method. You will doubtless feel, as I do, that he goes too far in his insistence that one should never give advice under any circumstances. This does not alter the fact that the book can help a minister, or anyone else, to know how to listen and how to accept the sufferer.

A third concept of psychotherapy is that the process of

mental healing cannot be accomplished by the person alone. We could help ourselves much better if we could see ourselves better, but for some reason it is not possible to see our deepest motives without assistance. For the person who is disturbed it seems completely impossible to do it alone. This is very hard to explain, and even harder to accept. People have great difficulty in believing they cannot see their hidden motives until they have been through the kind of experience that psychotherapy affords. So I will probably not convince my readers of it either, but I will point out that this is a rule of clinical psychology, and I believe it is a rule of the Bible which is clearly recognizable in James. We need each other. We cannot help ourselves nearly so well as we can help one another. It is jokingly said that psychoanalysts greet each other by saying, "You are fine. How am I?" The truth is that we must all do this. I cannot see myself as clearly as others see me, but in turn I am likely to see them better than they can see themselves. Our vision is complicated by severe blind spots in most of our lives; therefore it seems to me that a true psychoanalysis helps a person to see even himself much more clearly that he did before.

How We Can Promote Healing Among One Another

The perceptive reader already sees these concepts imbedded in James's treatment of healing. The sick person is to call the brethren. He could pray, and he should (5:13); but when he is sick he is supposed to call for others to pray with him too (5:14-16). There is individual responsibility here, but only up to a point. Unfortunately, it is at this point that too many people want to take all the responsibility and help themselves. Like Jonah, who fled from the commanded direction of Nineveh to go toward Tarshish, running our own lives will result only in troubles and the depth of despair. There is not only responsibility here, but responsibility to do the right thing. In fact, to call the brethren is to take the first step of faith. It is to recognize one's own incapacity, and James promises that *"God opposes the arrogant and gives grace to the humble"* (4:6, NEB).

James also says that we are to confess our faults one to another. It is true that we are to confess them to God. But just as in the matter of prayer we need the help of the brethren, so we are to confess one to another when we are sick — and perhaps at other times also. We are not asked to confess before the congregation but in the privacy of our homes, with a few trusted persons of approved quality. When one has committed a specific act against the congregation, then it is realistic to make amends to the church, but that is not the way to get at the deep personal problems which are at the root of neurosis. Public confession cannot possibly work except in a situation where one is in a sort of group therapy, with each person working through his own problem and nobody sitting by and listening — and James in no way suggests anything like group therapy. (Please notice that a public healing meeting has no resemblance to group therapy.)

Please notice also that the elders whom James mentions are to be good therapists in the sense that they accept the sick friend and his sins. There is no hint here of advice or admonition from the elders. They are to pray for the afflicted one. One does not pray for someone in this way unless he is known to have a problem. The elders evidently recognize that there is something worth praying about, but since the sick one has asked for help, there is no further need to judge what he has already judged by asking for help. He is already willing. He has not rebelled. The elders do the proper thing. They listen and pray.

I think I can hear them. I think they are saying something like this: "Lord, our brother has told us of his troubles, and of the imaginations of his heart, and of the things he has done. We believe that these are indeed a grievous and heavy burden for him. Lord, this is what he is. Now, Lord, you love him even more than we do, and you can forgive and help him to be cleared of this distress. We pray for him that he may be healed in his soul; that he may be able to grasp your outstretched, loving hand, and walk in a straight way because your love is his guide. Restore him to us whole, O Lord."

The performance of such a ceremony can seal the transaction between all involved and God. What matters is that the sufferer has faced the truth about himself, and has done it before sympathetic and qualified listeners. God can now be honestly drawn into the situation.

To those who ask if deep inner problems must always be brought out before another person, the answer of James and the answer of psychoanalysis is, "Definitely." There is no other way that works. Whether we call it sickness or sin (and James speaks about both in the same breath) it cannot be hidden nor forgotten. It must be brought into the open in the presence of a trusted human being, and it must be forgiven. This seems to be the method that God has chosen by the way in which He created us. James gives it to us by revelation, and Freud arrived at it by intellectual perception. There is every reason to believe that James was a very clear-headed observer himself.

James does not mention the Holy Spirit by name in his epistle, but that does not mean he leaves the Holy Spirit out of his thinking. He is telling us by what means the Holy Spirit can find access to our minds, and how He works in them. God has many specified methods through which He operates in us, such as prayer, confession, Bible reading, etc.

There is no magic in any of them, but since they are God-created channels of His gracious dealing with us, they are the methods He requires us to follow. I have no doubt that God created the structure of the human brain in such a way that His Holy Spirit could operate through it, and it is for this reason that the Bible is in part the "manual of operation" which the Manufacturer has sent with His complicated creation.

If we return now to James's image of the paradoxical God who is completely without deviation and yet generous and loving, we see that the old justice and grace paradox is very much present in this epistle also. However, in James we tend to see it from the human side rather than from God's side which is presented by the Apostle Paul. Man, who is torn by inner conflict, has not the faith with which to ask as he should, and therefore he cannot receive the very wisdom which he needs. Then of what value is it to know that God would be happy to grant his request if he only had faith? But here is God's second provision for man's redemption (having first given the substitutionary atonement of Christ for our sin and/or sickness) — the substitutionary petition of the saints for the sinner. God works in this way in order that He may remain just and yet be the justifier of all who come to Christ by the help of the saints (to state it in language parallel to that of Romans 3:26).

Thus it is that in the life of Jesus, ". . . some men brought him a paralytic lying on a bed. Seeing their faith Jesus said to the man, 'Take heart, my son; your sins are forgiven.' At this some of the lawyers said to themselves, 'This is blasphemous talk.' Jesus read their thoughts, and said, 'Why do you harbour these evil thoughts? Is it easier to say, "Your sins are forgiven," or to say, "Stand up and walk"? But to convince you that the

Son of Man has the right on earth to forgive sins' — he now addressed the paralytic — 'stand up, take your bed, and go home.' Thereupon the man got up, and went off home. The people were filled with awe at the sight, and praised God for granting such authority to men" (Matthew 9:2-8, NEB). In the same way our neurotic friend in the epistle of James calls upon a few righteous men to carry him, with a faith he cannot muster, to the immaculate throne of gracious gifts. *"The Lord will raise him from his bed, and any sins he may have committed will be forgiven."* (5:15, NEB).

Seeing this, some readers will doubtless say to themselves, "This is blasphemous talk; our sins are not forgiven because we confess to men." The Bible shows us, however, that there are different kinds of human ills, and that they need to be treated in different ways. In some instances we find that it is the faith of the sick person that makes him well. In other cases there is need for firm declarations of social evil and injustice. But in the sort of case James has in mind, the sin is forgiven when it is confessed before men, and the spirit and body are healed with it. The sufferer cannot muster enough faith alone.

Psychoanalysis gives careful and detailed treatment to the matter of this relationship between patient and the listening therapist, under the name of "transference." It is not possible to deal with this transference relationship more than we have already alluded to it, but it is important to know that through the transference relationship anxiety is dissolved, neurosis is cured, and psychosomatic healing does occur. We must leave it to the theologian to answer the question of whether such a professional relationship, with no religious overtones, results in God's forgiveness of the patient's sin. What we must observe here is that James carefully makes room for a similar relationship and experience. This being true, a wide door is opened for further exploration by Christians of the applicability of psychoanalytic techniques to double-mindedness and ambivalence, and the neuroses which result from them.

This is not to suggest that a short dissertation like this makes it possible for the reader to do deep psychotherapy. There are many more things to do than have been mentioned, and many skills to learn. But it is intended to suggest that if you will learn how to do this kind of listening and praying, many a case will never get so serious that it needs to come to the clinic or the hospital, and some of the less-involved illnesses will indeed disappear as "mysteriously" as they came.

It was a sad day when the Methodist "classes" grew so large and impractical that they were abandoned. There are movements everywhere, including the Methodist church, to bring back these small, intimate prayer and sharing groups. Today they can be improved with the help of knowledge which has been gained from group psychotherapy, to make them even more effective than they were before.

If each Christian listens well, we will help each other more than we can imagine. A good listener will listen well enough to know when the problem is of a sort too difficult for him to help, and then will have an opportunity to become the trusted friend who helps the sick one to more professional help. There will always be a need for physicians and psychologists, but there may never be enough of them to heal all the sick people. The church must return to its true healing ministry, and every Christian must become more skillful in his ability to listen, love and support. (There are other aspects of the church's healing ministry which are not included in James's epistle.) *"Therefore, confess your sins to one another, and pray for one another, and then you will be healed. A good man's prayer is powerful and effective"* (5:16, NEB).

Summary

The mind and body are interrelated in such a close and direct way that the illnesses of one affect the other. One may have physical illnesses which have physical causes (but are helped or hindered by the frame of mind); or one may have ailments which cause inconvenience, suffering, or incapacity, but for which no physical causes can be found; and one can have physical illnesses for which the primary cause is mental. The way in which this last relationship of sick mind and sick body is established is largely explained by the General Adaptation Syndrome.

When the faith of the sufferer is healed, the symptoms of the last two kinds of ailment are healed with it. Both James and psychoanalysis say that such a healing is accomplished by the method of having the sufferer ask for help from accepting and qualified persons, to whom he confesses his inner problem. Three specific therapeutic concepts are recognizable in James, namely, catharsis, acceptance by the listener, and the inability of the neurotic sufferer to understand or help himself.

In the kind of case with which James is dealing, both physical and spiritual restoration occur because of the faith of the assisting person, rather than from the efforts of the sick person alone. There are recognizable parallel concepts to those of psychoanalytic transference which were not discussed at length.

> *Is any sick among you? let him call for the elders of the church; and let them pray over him, anointing him with oil in the name of the Lord: And the prayer of faith shall save the sick, and the Lord shall raise him up; and if he have committed sins, they shall be forgiven him. Confess your faults one to another, and pray one for another, that ye may be healed. The effectual fervent prayer of a righteous man availeth much.* — James 5:14-16

8

THE MEEKNESS OF WISDOM —
THE "WAY" OF HEALTH

Who is wise and understanding among you? By his good life let him show his works in the meekness of wisdom. . . . the wisdom from above is first pure, then peaceable, gentle, open to reason, full of mercy and good fruits, without uncertainty or insincerity. And the harvest of righteousness is sown in peace by those who make peace.

— James 3:13, 17, RSV

There is a true popular saying that the great artist makes his art seem easy by its very perfection. Shakespeare says of the great personality characteristic,

> The quality of mercy is not strained,
> It droppeth as the gentle rain from heaven
> Upon the place beneath.

James says that true, modest, integrated self-control is "*first pure, then peaceable, gentle . . . ,* " and its gentle, natural fruit is righteousness.

Looking at the futility of ever trying to explain good personality with the use of words, the psychologist may well say with Joyce Kilmer, "Poems are made by fools like me," adding, "Only personality can make personality." The only seed that can really bring forth the fruit of righteousness is indeed that which is sown in peace by a peaceable person in the life of

153

another person. Yet psychologists go on writing books. It is comforting, however, to observe that even though God sent His Son as the final and full revelation of what He was trying to get across to mankind, yet He also gave the Book. Perhaps something can be communicated by words, little as that may be.

Personality Integration

In the words quoted above, James has given us his definition, in part, of personality integration. For the full picture, the entire book enters into the definition.

The wise person, as James calls him, has received his wisdom from above. That is, he has responded to the injunction of 1:5, has asked wisdom of God, and has received it. The elements of that wisdom are relevant to the theme of double-mindedness because they present the opposite, positive and single-minded personality.

This wisdom is first of all pure, and so it must be, for it was the admixture of the motives of the self which caused all the trouble in the first place. If one is to achieve wholeness, then this double-mindedness must be removed. The word "pure" in its basic definition means unmixed or unadulterated. The pure thing is just what it is intended to be, with no foreign presence. This is the condition of the person who has faced temptation and turned from it to walk in the Way, without deviation. It is possible to ponder on the word "pure" at length. I would certainly resist any interpretations which limit it to such special meanings as abstinence from specific popular pleasures or vices. It is a great deal more than that. It means freedom from anything whatsoever that could detract from the central purpose of the Christian.

Being pure, such wisdom is *"then peaceable, gentle,"* says James. These qualities are no signs of weakness, but an indication that the individual is not at all threatened by others, nor has any need to threaten others as a displacement for the divided, impure motives within himself. It is in the verses immediately following this that James speaks of the inwardly divided person as a quarreler.

Is there any better evidence of the "witness of the Spirit" within a person that he is a son of God, than that he has no need to defend himself before others? He is secure within himself, and he has no need to fight anything except real problems. It is no accident that Jesus, the brother of this writer, said, "Blessed are the peacemakers; for they shall be called the sons of God" (Matthew 5:9, RSV). In fact there is a striking resemblance between this list of personality attributes and the Beatitudes. The peacemakers are called the children of God for at least two reasons. One is the socially desirable results of their activities. The other is the psychological fact of the sort of integrated personality out of which peacemaking so easily arises as a natural expression. Like the artist, the integrated person makes it look easy because peacemaking is the unstrained expression of his true nature. Such a personality is the sound basis for the practice of biblical pacifism, reaching much deeper into the real issues involved in peacemaking than any mere attempt to regulate inter-personal relationships. As a man thinks in his heart, so is he.

The integrated person is also *"open to reason."* Indeed, until his ambivalence was resolved he could not reason in a straight line (1:8, NEB). We have already noticed that the disturbed person is driven by his emotional needs rather than by the facts of the situation. In one extreme form this drivenness is called "autistic thinking." The disturbed person sees things as he needs to see them rather than as they are. Since he is unable to face certain facts about himself, he is in the position of the engineer who has put into his multiplication table the falsehood that two times two makes a hopeful five, or like the artist who has eliminated red from his palette. The results are untrue to reality. To those who deal with them, these people seem to "reason in circles," "speak incoherently," "miss the point," or in some other way show themselves to be other than objective and rational. When the logician calls their errors by the correct classifications, or the clergymen calls them evil, they name the symptoms, but not the cause.

The wise person is also open to reason in the sense which one gets from the King James Version: he is *"easy to be entreated."* That such a person should be full of mercy is understandable, for love lives best with peace. In his recent book, *The Theory of Psychoanalytic Technique,* Menninger reverses the process of this book, and quotes from First Corinthians thirteen to illustrate what he regards as part of the final goal of psychoanalysis. The clearing out of the inner trash — the conflicts, guilts and fears — says Menninger, results in the ability to love and to be loved, among other things.

James is right in saying that such a person is *"full of . . . good fruits."* It is almost an etcetera added to the list, to indicate the full extent of this kind of life.

But the closing word of this list confirms again our original statement that the meekness of wisdom is a position of integrated and self-directed strength. James speaks of the wise person as being *"without uncertainty or insincerity."* It may be correct to say that sincerity is the outward expression of inward certainty. There is no need for the disguises and false, circular methods of neurosis. This person can be openly what he is inwardly.

Such people seem to have great inner resources. Actually, they may not have any more resources than others. They just don't waste them on intramural warfare.

Lest we be swept away with an incorrect idea, we must remember that integration can occur around other centers than the will of God, or the Way of Christianity. To point in a very opposite direction, Stalin was probably a very well-integrated person, and he exhibited a coordination of powers which might well have produced the Faust legend if it had not already existed.

Integration Around What?

There is a point here where we can see James leaving psychoanalytic theory and beginning to sound more like a Gestaltist. Personality integration is not an exact synonym for Christian personality. It is necessary to integrate around those things which the Bible teaches, in order for it to be Christian. Christianity is not only a matter of changing from double-mindedness to integration. There remains the question, "Integration around what focal point?"

We must never suppose that any one discipline can comprehend Christianity, for Christianity proposes to be as broad as life and all of creation. The psychologist can talk very meaningfully about methods by which certain things happen, and about the goals of a personality which can deal effectively with life, but much of the content of the Christian life must come from sources other than psychology. (And that happens to be good psychological theory.) In these chapters I have outlined what seems to me to be James's theory of neurotic defenses and of psychotherapy. But we must also look at what James expects of the personality if or when it is integrated.

What we have done thus far is somewhat comparable to the housecleaning of which Jesus speaks in the story of the evil spirit that left a man. When this man's house had been put in order, the same evil spirit, with seven others, returned and took possession. The common interpretation of this passage is that Jesus warned against leaving our mental and spiritual houses empty.

Therefore we are faced with an important consideration. It is not enough that one successfully employ a process or an experience. There must be a complete organizing meaning as well. That is, there must be content in the experience. One cannot have faith by itself; one must always have faith in something or someone that is worthy of such faith. It is not enough that one learn to think logically, for logical thinking can well be employed in crime; one must also think about what is good and right. It is not enough that one be converted, for conversion is a normal process of the human mind which can occur entirely outside of religion. One must be converted to the right thing. It is not enough that one be able to resolve double-mindedness. One must also have a true direction. Indeed, these should occur together. It is doubtless the inadequacy of the content of many Christian conversions that is a reason for much of the dissatisfaction we have with the results of conversion. The preacher is too often satisfied to spin the wheels of an emotional process, without insisting that one shall also arrive at an adequate destination. This leads me to say that all truly adequate evangelism must therefore be saturated with Bible teaching; and all true mental healing in which the church has an interest should either be combined with, or followed by, biblical teaching.

James does not make the mistake of dealing only with the emotional disturbance. So far, that is all we have talked about, according to the agreed topic for this book. We would fail both James and ourselves if we did not look at least briefly at some of his recommendations for the content of the Christian life.

The Way

It is surely of significance that the Protestant Reformation contained at least three major movements. One was centered on the rational aspects of the mind. That was the Calvinistic and Lutheran movement, which had as its watchword, "Faith." Another was centered upon the emotional aspects of the spirit of man. This was the Pietistic movement, of which the Methodist movement was a major part. This had as its watchword, "Experience." The third centered upon the effects of these other two on practical living. This was the Anabaptist movement, of which the modern Baptists, Mennonites, and Church of the Brethren are the direct heirs. Their watchword was "Life." These three movements were added to the elements of Protestantism which were carried over from the earlier church and from the Old Testament, elements which centered upon the transcendence of God in a special way. It is best represented today by the Episcopalians, and partly by the Lutherans. It tends to be sacramental, and its watchword is "Worship." To be sure, these are elements which are commonly found in some degree in all present-day Protestant churches, but they remain among the fairly distinct emphases. The epistle of James seems to recognize the legitimacy of each of these emphases in the complete Christian life.

The Christian life is not at all simple nor automatic. The Gospel may indeed be relatively simple in some ways, but no one can say that Christianity is. If it were as simple as some people try to make it, we would have no need for publishing houses, schools, colleges, commentaries, hymn books, denominations, or weekly Sunday school classes. We would get along very well with a few tape recordings of John 3:16. But we know that this is neither realistic nor possible. To do justice to all of the advice which James gives about the complete

Christian life requires at least all the commentaries that have been written on the epistle, plus the combined example of generations of wholesome Christian living. Let us give at least a nodding recognition to some of his admonition.

He says we are to ask for wisdom (1:5), and that we are to do it in faith, for the person who has no faith will receive nothing from God (1:6-8). The Calvinists will note that. He says that we are to submit to God and resist the devil (4:7), to weep and mourn wretchedly over our failure to perform God's will with our fellow men (3:9). The Pietists will certainly note that. For the Anabaptists he says that we are not to be merely hearers of the Word, but doers of it (1:22), we are to bridle our tongues (3:2-6), and to visit the widows and the orphans (1:27). The sacramentalists are remembered in the ceremonial anointing of the sick person with oil (5:14).

Such categorizing becomes cumbersome after a while. So let us merely list the rest: we are to humble ourselves in the sight of God (4:10), exercise patience (5:7), avoid grumbling (5:9), sing, pray (5:13), confess our sins to one another (5:16), pray for one another (5:16), and give financial assistance to those who are in need (2:14-17). We are to live by the law of liberty, in a whole-hearted and integratedly simple fulfilment of the Word of God. I like the way this last is expressed in the New English Bible; "*Away then with all that is sordid, and the malice that hurries to excess, and quietly accept the message planted in your hearts, which can bring you to salvation*" (1:21, NEB).

This kind of life requires faith, experience, life and devotion. Above all, it requires an honest evaluation of ourselves, and the ability to deal effectively with the internal conflicts which come when we are lured from the Way by our desires.

Salvation has many aspects. It is one thing to be accepted in the mind of God as one of His own redeemed children. It is another, though closely related thing, to have the hope of eternal life even beyond this physical life. It is still another thing, though still closely related, to be rescued from the evil of this age which seeks to make us do what we do not want to do. To be saved from the corroding effects of sin in this life may not be quite the same as to achieve peace of mind.

God wants all of these for us, not just some of them. An overemphasis or an omission can quickly become heresy, just as overemphases or omissions in the physical realm lead to illness. The Bible does not indicate that the purpose of God's salvation is fully satisfied when we have peace here and hell hereafter; nor when we have "hell" here and peace hereafter. The psychologist may be a little inclined to be satisfied with the first, and the Christian preacher with the latter.

Psychology and the Christian Life

If we have properly understood both the epistle of James and psychology and have properly brought them together, then we are farther along the way toward mental health with spiritual salvation. There must be no division in the personality. As the individual becomes increasingly possessed of his normal reasoning and feeling faculties, he becomes increasingly capable of, and in need of, something worthy to occupy the attention of those faculties.

There is a paragraph in Abraham Kaplan's article in the *Saturday Evening Post* which seems to fit at this juncture.

> Mental health is the point of departure for religion, not its destination. . . . Psychoanalysis remains essentially as Freud conceived it — an attempt to help the patient realize his capacity to love and create. When the analyst finishes, it is up to the patient to use these new-found capacities, and in doing so he may achieve true religious faith. Religion begins where therapy leaves off, or rather religion works through what health is given us. It takes a healthy

maturity to see all things as miraculous and the world as revelation. Religion culminates in that sense of awe in which the Greeks saw the birth of philosophy, and in which Judaism and Christianity find the life of the spirit.[1]

Although I would argue that Christianity has more to offer in the way of mental hygiene and therapy than Dr. Kaplan indicates, it is interesting to see to what extent a recognized psychoanalyst finds himself in a team with the clergy.

With no intention of "baptizing psychoanalysis" (which I think is an idea repugnant to both sides), I hope this book has nevertheless pointed out several things: that there are some interesting and important ways in which the psychoanalytic approach to mental illness parallels that of the Bible; that one does not need to accept or reject psychoanalytic theory on an all-or-nothing basis; and that there are some important distinctions between the mental processes of the human being, and the content with which those processes work.

Let me repeat that there are a number of other major psychological theories of personality, and other psychological methods which apply to various aspects of human experience and behavior. If they have been largely omitted from this book it is not because I do not believe them to be valid, but because, within the brief scope of this study it is not possible to write a complete psychological commentary on even so brief a passage as the epistle of James.

It is my hope that this incomplete presentation of psychoanalytic theory of ambivalence in neurosis coupled with this limited commentary on the epistle of James will provide for the Christian reader some new insights into the resources which are available to him for a fuller inheritance of God's intended blessings — both in the Bible and in psychotherapy.

---

[1]Abraham Kaplan, "Psychiatrists and Clergymen: Enemies or Allies?" *The Saturday Evening Post*, Sept. 23, 1961.

GLOSSARY

GLOSSARY

aggression Behavior which is designed to drive away or destroy. It is also sometimes used in a manner which is not hostile, but denotes a pushing of one's own interests or ideas.

  libidinal aggression A psychoanalytic term which refers to the natural, unrefined, instinctual hostile action in defense of one's own interests, without thought or plan.

  displaced aggression Aggression against a person or object other than the cause of the original FRUSTRATION.

  self-displaced aggression Aggression against oneself, usually in a destructive manner, instead of against the source of FRUSTRATION.

ambivalence A psychological pull in opposite, unreconcileable directions at the same time.

anxiety There are a number of theories of anxiety. The one used in this book is: a fear, usually of relatively low intensity and long duration, regarding some inadequacy of the personality which is not available to CONSCIOUSNESS, and therefore cannot be consciously dealt with.

autistic thinking Thinking which is so introverted and self-directed that it ignores reality and perceives objects and events only in the light of personal needs and desires.

behavioristic school of psychology A theoretical position proposed early in the 20th century by John B. Watson and others, which has undergone considerable modification since that time. Some of the essential principles are that all human behavior is the result of learning by way of biologically determined processes; thus there is no inborn set of ideas or instincts, and there is no free will. Human behavior can thus be changed by simply manipulating the correct circumstances, in accordance with learning principles.

catharsis Literally, purging. In PSYCHOLOGY it refers to reliving or relating materials from one's past which are troublesome to the PERSONALITY.

clinical psychologist A PSYCHOLOGIST who specializes in working with emotional problems of people.

SMALL CAPITALS indicate cross references.

clinical psychology That specialty within PSYCHOLOGY that concerns itself primarily with human emotional problems. It overlaps with counseling psychology, and is usually distinguished by the rule-of-thumb that clinical psychology treats more severe emotional problems over longer periods of time, and with more intensive methods. Thus a clinical psychologist frequently works in a mental hospital, counseling psychologists seldom do.

compulsion A force that causes a person to act against his inclination. In PSYCHOLOGY, the force comes from within the person, is not under his control, and usually drives the person to behavior that is more or less unpleasant.

conscience The sense of moral, ethical or religious goodness or blame-worthiness of one's behavior or motives.

consciousness Self-awareness.

conversion In any sense it means a change or turning from one position to another. In PSYCHOLOGY the term is not used alone, but in the term "CONVERSION REACTION."

conversion reaction In PSYCHOLOGY this is a specialized term referring to the process of changing an emotional problem into a physical problem. This is always accomplished unconsciously, so that the person is aware of the results, but not of the fact that he has achieved them by this means.

displacement In PSYCHOLOGY this refers to the process, accomplished unconsciously, of changing the emotional response to something which is not the cause of the response.

ego There are several meanings, all of them referring to "the self." In this book we use the term to mean the thinking, rational, disciplined, self-conscious self.

emotional illness A disturbance in the normal function of the mental and/or emotional processes of a person.

experimental psychologist A PSYCHOLOGIST who specializes in empirical research. This usually refers to research with animals of the biological aspects involved in human learning and behavior.

experimental psychology That specialization within PSYCHOLOGY that concentrates on empirical research, especially with animals or the biological aspects of human learning and behavior.

SMALL CAPITALS indicate cross references.

frustration   The blocking of a goal.

Gestalt   A German word meaning form or configuration. Used in PSYCHOLOGY to designate that whole characteristic of something which is more than the total of its parts. As, for instance, a tune is a gestalt which cannot be explained by enumerating the notes, time sequences and other elements of which it is composed.

Gestaltist   A person who adheres to the psychological position, founded by Max Wertheimer, which teaches that human experience and behavior is not essentially composed of unrelated bits, but of meaningful wholes which are more than the addition of the elements of experience.

hypochondria   A NEUROTIC characteristic of being preoccupied by vague, but persistent impressions that one is ill.

hypochondriacal symptoms   Symptoms of illness which are not based on actual tissue damage, but upon the need of the patient to discover some illness in himself.

hysteria   A NEUROTIC characteristic of reproducing the specific symptoms of an ailment and experiencing them as though they were physically present. Like all neurotic processes this is accomplished unconsciously.

hysteric symptoms   These are the symptoms of a specific ailment, experienced as real by the patient, but in the absence of any tissue damage or disease.

integration   Used variously in PSYCHOLOGY, but in this book it means fitting all the motives and behavior of an individual into an idea-system and behavior which are mutually helpful, and which achieve the best possible welfare of all the person's interests over the long term.

irrational   Not rational, logical, or reasonable. Contrary to reason.

mental health   The state of normal mental facility and function.

mental illness   A state of disturbance of normal mental facility or function. Not to be confused with mental retardation, which is a lack of native capacity for intellectual function.

neurasthenic   A condition characterized by a general lack of vitality and healthiness, but without prominent identifiable

SMALL CAPITALS indicate cross references.

symptoms, which is a NEUROTIC reaction to psychological stress which the individual cannot master.

neurosis   A mental disorder more mild than psychosis, and generally distinguished from PSYCHOSIS in that it does not cause the person to become detached from reality or the ability to relate emotionally.

neurotic   adj. Having the characteristics of neurosis. *n* A person who exhibits the characteristics of neurosis.

obsession   A thought that forces itself into consciousness, against the will of the person, is usually unpleasant, and cannot be dismissed by an action of the will.

personality   There are many definitions of the term, but we use it here to refer to the sum total of what a person is.

phobia   An IRRATIONAL fear.

projection   The process of attributing one's own attributes or motives to someone else.

psychiatrist   A physician who practices PSYCHIATRY. A psychiatrist must have an M.D. degree.

psychiatry   A specialization within medicine that deals with emotional disorders. Psychiatry and CLINICAL PSYCHOLOGY overlap. The psychiatrist has a medical degree and the CLINICAL PSYCHOLOGIST does not, hence the clinical psychologist does not dispense drugs nor do surgery.

psychoanalysis   A theory of PERSONALITY and method of dealing with MENTAL ILLNESS which was originated by Sigmund Freud, and has undergone considerable development since he introduced it late in the 19th century.

psychoanalyst   A person who practices the special method of dealing with MENTAL ILLNESSES which is called psychoanalysis.

psychologist   A person who is professionally engaged in one of the many specialized areas of psychology, such as educational psychology, industrial psychology, EXPERIMENTAL PSYCHOLOGY, CLINICAL PSYCHOLOGY, etc.

psychology   The science of human behavior. It differs from other social sciences in that it is concerned with what goes on within

SMALL CAPITALS indicate cross references.

the individual rather than what happens between individuals or in groups of individuals.

psychoneurotic   A synonym for NEUROTIC.

psychosis   Severe MENTAL ILLNESS, characterized by loss of contact with reality, loss of appropriate emotional reaction to life situations, and other severely disabling disruptions of mental and emotional life.

psychotic behavior   Behavior of a person who has PSYCHOSIS.

psychosomatic   Referring to the interrelationship of the body and the mind, as in psychosomatic illness.

psychotherapy   Any method of healing which uses psychological methods rather than physical methods.

group psychotherapy   A form of treatment of emotional or mental disturbance in which a small group of persons meet with a psychotherapist and interact under his direction. Several kinds of THERAPY are employed in group situations.

rational   Based on or consistent with reason.

reaction-formation   The process of feeling or behaving in a manner opposite to a person's real inclination. The change occurs unconsciously, and the person believes the opposite feeling or behavior to be genuine.

repression   The process of blocking from availability to CONSCIOUSNESS material which is unpleasant.

Rorschach test   A technique for PERSONALITY evaluation which was devised by the Swiss PSYCHIATRIST Herman Rorschach. It is popularly recognized as the technique in which the subject is shown ink blots and asked to tell what they look like.

scapegoating   The process of blaming an innocent person for FRUSTRATIONS which really have another source. Like other DISPLACEMENTS, the person who does this is unconscious of the real source of frustration. The word comes from the Old Testament practice of symbolically putting the sins of the people on a goat and banishing it into the desert.

stress   Any force or strain that is applied to the PERSONALITY, or to the body.

SMALL CAPITALS indicate cross references.

sublimation The process of changing one's original, unattainable goal into a similar attainable goal which is socially and personally acceptable. This is a wholesome DISPLACEMENT process, and is accomplished unconsciously.

suppression Consciously restraining feelings, thoughts or actions.

sympathetic and parasympathetic nervous systems A classification of the nervous system according to their function. In this book the significant aspect of these systems is that they work opposite each other. Among other things the parasympathetic system causes the constriction of the pupils, dilation of the blood vessels, slowing the heart, and increasing the activity of the glands and the digestive system. The sympathetic system, speeds up the heart, etc.

syndrome The pattern of symptoms which is characteristic of an ailment, and by which the ailment can be recognized.

General Adaptation Syndrome A pattern of reactions, especially of the endocrine gland system which protects the body from any kind of STRESS which is too great to be easily accommodated, but not great enough to cause quick death. Among the stresses which have been found to create this syndrome are poisons, diseases, and psychological disturbances. The syndrome was discovered and described by Hans Selye, M.D.

therapy Any kind of treatment which is intended to cure any kind of ailment. See PSYCHOTHERAPY.

transference The process of feeling and behaving toward the therapist in the way one felt or behaved toward significant persons in one's early development, even though the feelings and behavior are inappropriate at this time.

Unconscious, the In PSYCHOANALYTIC theory of the personality, the Unconscious (capitalized) is the part of the PERSONALITY which is not accessible to the conscious and RATIONAL part of the personality, but which is nevertheless very influential in the affairs of the personality because it is the source of much instinctual motivation and is also the storehouse of repressed material (SEE REPRESSION).

SMALL CAPITALS indicate cross references.

INDEX TO SCRIPTURE REFERENCES

INDEX TO SCRIPTURE REFERENCES

INDEX

INDEX

(does not include glossary page numbers)

A

Achan, 46
Abnormal Psychology and Modern Life, Coleman, 73*n*, 77*n*
Abraham, 46
Academy of Religion and Mental Health, 14
acceptance, 21
  in healing ministry, 131–132, 147
  in psychotherapy, 144–145
Adam, 21, 136
adrenal cortex, 140, 142
aggression
  creatively transformed, 97–99
  causes of, 95–102
  displaced, 97ff.
  and juvenile delinquents, 97
  libidinal, 96
  self-displaced, 109ff.
alcoholics, 109
Alcoholics Anonymous, 124
alcoholism, 124
ambivalence
  in behavior, 66ff.
  defined, 50
  and demon possession, 115
  and double-mindedness, 50, 70ff.
  of emotion, 32, 32*n*, 43*n*, 67ff., 76, 121
  and faith, 138
  four kinds of, 75–60
  illustration of, 49
  involves self-torture and self-hatred, 92, 109
  and neurotic compulsions, 120–121, 132
  produces anxiety, 73ff., 83ff.
  produces war, (94ff.), 108, 111–112
  result of inner conflict, 44f., 50
  results in confused thinking, 60ff., 69–70, 74
  results in repression, 60ff.
  results in self-defeat, 67ff.
  sources of, 73ff.
  and suicide, 109–110
  unresolved, 83ff., 89, 111

  see also double-mindedness, neurosis, personality conflict
America
  churches in, 109
  psychologists in, 13
American Association for the Advancement of Science, 14
American Association of Pastoral Counselors, 16
American Psychological Association, 14
American Scientific Affiliation, 16
Americans, 31, 100, 101
Anabaptist movement, 159ff.
Anabaptists, 160
anger, 47, 64
  continuous, and body stress, 140–141
  displacement of, 100ff.
  illustration of, 61–62
  of juvenile delinquents, 96
  and projection, 107
  and reaction-formation, 104ff.
  transformed, 98–99
  vented in scapegoating, 100ff.
Answer to Job, Jung, 20
anthropology, 16
anxiety, 31
  arises from inner conflicts, 73–83, 93
  difference between fear and, 83, 93
  free-floating, 85
  handled by reaction forming, 104–105
  neurotic transformation of, 85ff., 93
  produced by repressed material, 83ff.
  and scapegoating, 112
appendicitis, 87, 137
art, 11, 15, 153
Augustine, Saint, 28
autistic thinking, 155–156
autopsy, 141

177

M